Necessary War

What America Needs to Know About the War in Afghanistan

Paul D. Miller

ISBN: 0615691838
ISBN-13: 978-0615691831

Political Science / International Relations / General

DEDICATION

This is dedicated to the men and women of the United States Armed Forces who gave of their time and their lives in the service of a just and necessary war.

CONTENTS

PERMISSIONS

Chapter 2 is adapted from an article first published in the *World Affairs Journal* ("It's Not Just al-Qaeda: Stability in the World's Most Dangerous Region," March/April 2012, pg. 63-73), which authorized republication herein. All rights are retained by World Affairs. www.worldaffairsjournal.org.

Chapter 3 is adapted by permission of *First Things* from "Justice and the War in Afghanistan," scheduled to appear in December 2012 or January 2013.

Chapter 4 is reprinted by permission of *Foreign Affairs* from "Finish the Job: How to Win the War in Afghanistan," January/February 2011, Vol. 90, No. 1, pg. 51-65. Copyright 2011 by the Council on Foreign Relations, Inc. www.ForeignAffairs.com.

Chapter 5 was previously published in *The Washington Quarterly* as "How to Exercise U.S. Leverage Over Pakistan," Vol. 35, Issue 4, Fall 2012.

The views and errors in this book are my own. All statements of fact, opinion, or analysis expressed are mine and do not reflect the official positions of the U.S. Army, the Department of Defense, the White House, the Central Intelligence Agency, either Administration for which I worked, or any other organization or agency. Nothing in the contents should be construed as asserting or implying U.S. Government authentication of information or endorsement of the author's views. This material has been reviewed by the CIA and the National Defense University to prevent the disclosure of classified information.

1 MYTHS OF WAR

I served in Afghanistan with the U.S. Army in 2002. I then worked as a political analyst with the CIA's Office of South Asian Analysis from 2003 to 2007. When President George W. Bush appointed Lieutenant General Doug Lute as his "war czar," Lute hired me as one of his Directors for Afghanistan on the National Security Council staff (I and the other directors jokingly called ourselves "war serfs"). I worked in the White House in that capacity through September 2009, supporting the Bush administration's Afghanistan-Pakistan strategy review of 2008, the presidential transition, and the Obama administration's Afghanistan-Pakistan strategy review in the spring of 2009. Currently, I teach at the National Defense University, at which I developed and direct the College of International Security Affairs' South and Central Asia Program and help educate the U.S. military's "Af-Pak Hands."

This collection of essays argues that the war in Afghanistan is important (chapter 2), just (chapter 3), and winnable (chapter 4). It lays out a strategy for how to complete the mission there by cracking down on Pakistan (chapter 5) and establishing a lasting commitment to Afghan security and governance (chapter 6).

My argument is straightforward. Before I get to it, I need to raise and refute some common objections to the war. These objections are based, in my view, on myths that have grown up around the war and the country. They are potent myths that get in the way of a clear argument about the United States' interests in Afghanistan and our prospects for success there.

Myth: *Afghanistan is America's longest war.*
Fact: The United States' 11-year involvement in Afghanistan is its longest war only to people unaware of American history or the definition of war.

The United States has not been at war for the full 11 years of its involvement in Afghanistan. From March 2002 to mid-2005, political violence was infrequent, disorganized, and rarely killed people—almost certainly fewer than 1,000 people per year were killed on all sides from combat-related causes, the conventional threshold of "war."

But even if you count the Afghan war as lasting 11 years, it is still not America's longest war or intervention. The United States fought a longer campaign in the Philippines (1899 – 1913). It undertook a much longer armed intervention in Haiti (1915-1934), and the full stretch of U.S. involvement in Vietnam lasted from 1954 to 1973. U.S. Army historians treat the Army's various 19th Century campaigns in the American West as the "Indian Wars" stretching from 1865 to 1890.

The mantra that Afghanistan is America's longest war is nakedly false.

Myth: *We can't afford the war in Afghanistan.*
Fact: The war in Afghanistan is the second-cheapest major war in American history, according to the Congressional Research Service,[1] and it is not the main driver of U.S. fiscal deficits. From 2001 to 2010, the war accounted for about 1 percent of U.S. federal expenditures. In the same time frame, about 65 percent of federal expenditures went towards entitlements, about 15 percent went towards national defense, excluding the wars in Iraq and Afghanistan. Iraq cost three percent.[2] The

United States spends about as much on the war in Afghanistan each year as it does on the Department of Housing and Urban Development.

Myth: *The U.S. doesn't have a clear goal or strategy.*
Fact: President Obama clearly defined U.S. goals for Afghanistan and how to achieve them.

President Obama said on March 27, 2009, "we have a clear and focused goal: to disrupt, dismantle and defeat al Qaeda in Pakistan and Afghanistan, and to prevent their return to either country in the future." In December he specified what it would take to prevent al Qaida's return to Afghanistan. He said that "We must reverse the Taliban's momentum and deny it the ability to overthrow the government. And we must strengthen the capacity of Afghanistan's Security Forces and government, so that they can take lead responsibility for Afghanistan's future." He outlined a strategy—echoed in ISAF Commanding General Stanley McChrystal's operational plan—to combine military efforts against the Taliban with civilian efforts to bolster the Afghan government.

Nor was President Obama's strategy entirely new. He clarified, made explicit, and devoted more resources to the strategy that had gradually been taking shape since 2007. President Bush had clearly committed U.S. forces to preventing the Taliban's conquest of the country and training new Afghan security forces. He deployed an additional 20,000 U.S. troops to Afghanistan between the end of 2006 and the end of 2008. And in a single year, from 2006 to 2007, Bush nearly quadrupled U.S. funding for Afghan security forces from $1.9 billion to $7.4 billion. President Bush also incorporated an explicit, if uneven and under-resourced, civilian component to his Afghanistan strategy. Bush said in an April 2002 speech at the Virginia Military Institute that "We know that true peace will only be achieved when we give the Afghan people the means to achieve their own aspirations. Peace will be achieved by helping Afghanistan develop its own stable government," words he put into effect with support to the Bonn Process and elections in 2004 and 2005. Bush failed to recognize that elections are necessary but not sufficient ingredients in a civilian strategy, something the Obama Administration has sought to correct.

While the U.S. does have a clear goal and strategy, it lacks time. Because the strategy has taken shape and been given proper resources only recently, it may be years yet before it begin to show consistent effects. Counterinsurgency and statebuilding require patience.

Myth: *Afghanistan has always been violent and badly ungoverned.*
Fact: Afghanistan was relatively stable for most of its history prior to 1978.

Civil war, insurgency, drug trafficking, extremism, rampant corruption, and utter state failure did not characterize Afghanistan until 1978, and for the most part not until the end of the Soviet war in 1989. Before that Afghanistan was certainly poor and rarely democratic, but it did not reach the depths of failure and bloodshed that have characterized Afghanistan in recent decades.

Afghanistan endured foreign invasion, civil war, and Taliban autocracy between 1978 and 2001—a succession of shocks and destruction unparalleled in Afghan history, or few other countries' histories. The perfect storm of highly unique circumstances destroyed the Afghan state and created the most completely failed state on earth. Afghans turned to drug trafficking and massive corruption only when licit economic opportunity was destroyed by endemic war in the 1980s and 1990s.

The extent of state failure, violence, and criminality in Afghanistan today is an aberration, not the norm. A cartoonish or caricatured version of Afghan history is no grounds to justify despair in the current effort.

Myth: *Afghans are xenophobic and always resist foreign intervention.*
Fact: Afghans are legendary for the hospitality, not their xenophobia. Afghans do indeed resist foreign invasions—but

who doesn't? Afghans fought and lost two small colonial wars against the United Kingdom (1839-1842 and 1878-1880), and only won a third (1919) because the United Kingdom was bankrupt and exhausted after World War I. Afghans nearly lost the Soviet war (1979-1989) and only won when it became a full-fledged proxy war pitting the Soviet Union against the combined arms and money of the United States and the Muslim world.

Afghans overwhelmingly welcomed international intervention in 2001. Afghans continued to register strong support for foreign assistance from the United States, the United Nations, and coalition partners for years afterwards. Westerners are fond of comparing the current effort to British imperialism and Soviet invasion, but the only Afghans who do so are the Taliban. The rest, apparently, can tell the difference.

Myth: *Afghanistan is the graveyard of empires.*
Fact: As Thomas Barfield writes, "While the popular press often repeats the claim that no conqueror, including such figures as Alexander the Great or Chinggis Khan, ever succeeded in subduing the country, this is untrue. Most of these figures did subjugate the lands that now comprise Afghanistan and then occupied the territory they had won. [Parts of Afghanistan] were component parts of larger empires [who] had their centers in Iran (Achaemenid, Parthian, Sassanian, Seljukid, Il khanate, Safavid, and Afgharid), India (Mauryah and Mughal), or central Asia (Mongol, Timurid, and Uzbek)."[3]

Myth: *Building a modern state in Afghanistan is unnecessary and impossible.*
Fact: Statebuilding is key to lasting success, and there are more examples of it than you think.

The United States tried to skimp on statebuilding in Afghanistan from 2001 to 2006 or so, and that is exactly what created the challenges in Afghanistan today. The insurgency and drug trade were able to escalate out of control precisely because there was no functioning Afghan state to stop them. Afghans must have the tools to protect their own borders, uphold basic public order, and enforce laws or al Qaida will easily be able to regain a safe haven in Afghanistan. Statebuilding is the necessary path to sustainable security.

Democracy, statebuilding, and peacebuilding are also not as rare or as "western" as critics say. Democracy has successfully grown in nonwestern societies. There are 33 states in the world outside of Europe and North America that hold regular, competitive elections. Afghans themselves held somewhat free and fair democratic elections—in *1965* and *1969*, without any foreign pressure or aid. Nor is there anything particularly western about the ministries, central bank, prisons, army, law courts, or administrative offices the U.S. is trying to build. And the international community has become increasingly successful in helping societies recover after war. Since the Cold War the United Nations and its partners have seen varying degrees of successful peacebuilding in Namibia, Mozambique, Nicaragua, El Salvador, Guatemala, Bosnia, Croatia, Kosovo, East Timor, and Sierra Leone.

2 WHY AFGHANISTAN MATTERS

In 2002 only six percent of Americans believed it was a mistake to send military forces to Afghanistan.[1] Today, Osama bin Laden is dead, U.S. forces marked their eleventh anniversary in Afghanistan, and a growing number of voices are arguing that it is time to withdraw. Days after bin Laden's death, Senator John Kerry (D-MA) wrote that, "Duty calls at home." Conservative commentator Larry Kudlow echoed much of the media when he asked, post-Osama, "What exactly are we doing in Afghanistan?" And foreign policy expert Les Gelb argued that "the original mission [in Afghanistan] is accomplished" and other missions are peripheral to American interests. The public seems inclined to agree. By 2012 six percent had grown to 39 percent, almost half believed the war was going poorly, and President Obama announced the first withdrawals of American troops from Afghanistan in 2011.

Is it time to go? What, after all, have the United States and the international community been trying to accomplish there? Does the United States have enduring interests in the region that would justify not only the last decade of blood and treasure, but an enduring presence for years to come? President Obama in his first year in office offered only a narrow definition of U.S. goals: "to disrupt, dismantle, and defeat al Qaeda in Pakistan and Afghanistan, and to prevent their return to either country in the future." While the focus on counterterrorism is understandable, Obama inadvertently fell into the trap usually ascribed to his predecessor: he centered U.S. foreign policy in South Asia entirely on counterterrorism to the exclusion of other considerations.

Obama's policy ignores the United States' broader interests in South Asia. The success or failure of the war in Afghanistan will affect all of America's interests across South Asia: Pakistan's stability, the security of its nuclear weapons, NATO's credibility, relations with Iran and Russia, transnational drug-trafficking networks, worldwide democracy, and humanitarian considerations.

These real and enduring interests require a substantial and lasting commitment to the region and they explain why the mission in Afghanistan is not simply to deny safe haven to al-Qaida, but to foster lasting stability in Afghanistan. If Afghanistan falls into chaos again, al-Qaida or similar groups will reestablish a base there. Pakistan—and its nuclear weapons—will be less safe. Russia and Iran, two of America's rivals, will expand their influence. NATO, a pillar of American security, will be critically weakened. Transnational organized crime and drug trafficking will find a safe headquarters for business. The experiment of democracy in the Muslim world will be tarnished. And a humanitarian catastrophe will unfold in South Asia.

Thus, the U.S.-led mission is not simply to destroy al-Qaida or deny it safe haven. It is also to rebuild and stabilize Afghanistan. This mission has been plagued with difficulty because Presidents Bush and Obama failed to understand, articulate, plan, or resource this mission adequately. Obama (or his successor) should reformulate U.S. strategy and goals in South Asia, take into account the full range of U.S. interests, and explain to the American people and the world why an enduring commitment to the region is necessary.

Al-Qaida Delenda Est

Both Presidents Bush and Obama rightly stressed that the first and most important reason that the United States is involved Afghanistan is to deny safe haven to al-Qaida and other like-minded terrorist groups. Safe haven gives terrorists space, time, and stability to train, plan, fundraise, and establish reliable command and control over a global network. It crucially enhances their capabilities across the board. The existence of anti-American terrorists of global reach with safe haven in an entire country governed by a hostile regime represents an unacceptable risk to American national security. That is the first and most important reason why the United States in engaged in Afghanistan.

The Afghanistan Study Group, a collection of scholars and former policymakers critical of the current intervention, argued in 2010 that al-Qaida is no longer in Afghanistan and is unlikely to return, even if Afghanistan reverts to chaos or Taliban rule. It argued that three things must happen for al-Qaida to reestablish safe haven and threaten the United States. "1) the Taliban must seize control of a substantial portion of the country, 2) Al Qaeda must relocate there in strength, and 3) it must build facilities in this new 'safe haven' that will allow it to plan and train more effectively than it can today." But because all three are unlikely to happen, the Study Group argued, al-Qaida almost certainly will not reestablish a presence in Afghanistan in a way that threatens U.S. security. "Each of these three steps is unlikely, however, and the chances of all three together are very remote."[2]

In fact, none of those three steps are necessary for al-Qaida to regain safe haven and threaten America. The first premise is simply untrue: al-Qaida could return to Afghanistan even if the Taliban do not. It could—and probably would—find safe haven there if Afghanistan relapsed into chaos or civil war. Militant groups, including al-Qaida off-shoots, have gravitated towards other failed states, like Somalia and Yemen, because the absence of law and order is a permissive environment for them. Afghanistan would be especially tempting because they already know the terrain and have local connections. It is extremely unlikely that al-Qaida, faced with Somalia-like anarchy in Afghanistan and only a residual American military force there, would forgo the opportunity to set up their old shop. Afghanistan might escape the Taliban threat yet still become an inviting target for al-Qaida if it simply collapses or fails to reestablish basic public order. Second, al-Qaida does not need to return to Afghanistan "in strength" to be a threat. Terrorist operations, including the attacks of 2001, are typically planned and carried out by very few people. Al-Qaida will never again operate in any country on as large a scale or as openly as it did in Afghanistan before 2001—locals fearful of American retaliation would not let it—but it does not need to do so in order to be a threat.

This argument matters because the international community needs to deny safe haven *permanently*, not just so long as there is a large international military presence there. If al-Qaida is unlikely to return whether the Taliban win or lose, then the United States has already accomplished its most important goal in Afghanistan and could have withdrawn years ago. But if, as I argue, al-Qaida or like-minded groups would return if given the chance, the international community should not withdraw until there is an Afghan government and Afghan security forces with the will and capacity to deny safe haven without international help. Denying safe haven to al-Qaida requires stabilizing Afghanistan as a necessary precondition.

The Strategic Prize: Pakistan

The United States is also involved in Afghanistan to prevent the Taliban from destabilizing Pakistan. Policymakers do not often publicly admit this is a goal of U.S. policy in South Asia for fear of offending Pakistani officials sensitive to the implication that their country is unstable, but it is plainly true. Pakistan is a nuclear-armed Islamic state, the sixth-most-populous country in the world, and one of the larger developing Asian economies after China and India. It is a long-standing ally of the United States, dating back to the early days of the Cold War, and President Bush designated it a Major Non-Nato Ally in 2004. State failure in Pakistan could mean chaos and civil war in one of the world's largest countries, and it could mean a loss of control of Pakistan's nuclear weapons. Preventing state failure in Pakistan is a vital national interest of the United States.

Alarmingly, Pakistan is approaching the brink of civil war. A collection of militant Islamist groups, including al-Qaida, Tehrik-e Taliban Pakistan (TTP), and Tehrik-e Nafaz-e Shariat-e Mohammadi (TNSM), among others, have fought a growing insurgency in that has escalated dramatically in since 2007 across Khyber Pakhtunkhwa, the Federally Administered Tribal Areas, and Baluchistan. According to the Brookings Index on Pakistan, insurgents, militants, and terrorists now regularly launch more than 150 attacks on Pakistani government, military, and infrastructure targets per month, and have been for at least the last three years. Pakistan has deployed nearly 100,000 regular army soldiers to its western provinces—to combat fellow Pakistanis, not to counter an external threat. Nearly 3,000 soldiers have been killed in combat with militants since 2007.[3] Militants have been able to seize control of whole towns and districts. In 2007 Pakistani militants assassinated Benazir Bhutto, a candidate for Prime Minister, and nearly shut down Pakistan's capital city when they seized control of the Red Mosque in downtown Islamabad. In 2009 militants briefly seized control of a district just 40 miles outside of the capital. Tens of thousands of Pakistani civilians and militants—the distinction between which is not always clear—have been killed in daily insurgent and counterinsurgent operations. Pakistan is facing its gravest domestic crisis since the Civil War of 1971 sundered the country in two and changed the map of South Asia.

Pakistan's collapse or fall to Islamist militants is unlikely, but the implications of that scenario are so dire that they cannot be ignored. Even short of a collapse, increasing chaos and instability in Pakistan could give cover for terrorists to train, plan, or attempt to steal a nuclear weapon. The group is also a threat to the United States: Faisal Shahzad, the Pakistani-American who attempted to detonate a car bomb in New York's Times Square in 2010, was trained in explosives and given funding by the Pakistani Taliban.[4] And Pakistani officials told Secretary of State Hillary Clinton in October that they were unable to prioritize action against the Haqqani Network, which is responsible for attacks against U.S. personnel in Afghanistan, because the Pakistani military was overstretched fighting Pakistani militants.

The two insurgencies in Afghanistan and Pakistan are linked. Defeating the Afghan Taliban would give the United States and Pakistan momentum in the fight against the Pakistani Taliban, and vice versa. A Taliban takeover in Afghanistan, on the other hand, will give new strength to the Pakistani insurgency. The Pakistani insurgency would gain an ally in Kabul, safe haven to train and from which to launch attacks into Pakistan, and a huge morale boost in seeing their compatriots win power in a neighboring country. The two insurgencies are part of a single theater of war, stem from a single worldview and inspiration, and together pose an unacceptable threat to American interests. The Afghan insurgency is stronger and more coherent, but the Pakistani one is undoubtedly the greater long-term threat. Failure in Afghanistan would make stability in Pakistan much harder to maintain.

The Great Game

The fate of Afghanistan will have repercussions beyond Pakistan. Afghanistan lies between Iran and Pakistan, borders China, and is within reach of Russia and India. It sits on the crossroads between Asia's great powers. Two of these powers are especially troublesome for the United States in South Asia: Russia and Iran. Both are revisionist powers that seek to establish unwanted influence over their neighbors. Both are aggressive in subtle and, sometimes, overt ways. Iran is seeking to build nuclear weapons and uses the terrorist group Hezbollah as a proxy to bully neighboring countries and threaten Israel. Russia under Vladimir Putin is seeking to reestablish autocracy and home and its sphere of influence over its "near-abroad," in pursuit of which it (probably) cyber-attacked Estonia in 2007, invaded Georgia in 2008, and imprisoned and assassinated domestic dissidents like Mikhail Khodorkovsky and Alexander Litvinenko, respectively.

As it did during the Cold War with the Soviet Union, the United States should pursue a strategy to contain and limit the influence of Russia and Iran. The United States is not at war with either state, but is rightly suspicious of both. They both have articulated motives for opposing the United States' foreign policy agenda, either because it is the "Great Satan," or because it supposedly is working to preserve its hegemony and forestall multipolarity. If either state amassed too much power—for example, if Iran acquired nuclear weapons or Russia revived its domination of Eastern European and Central Asian energy supplies and markets—they would match their motives with the means for threatening the United States, its allies, and Americans' way of life. Preventing the growth of Russian and Iranian influence is a vital interest of the United States.

Central and South Asia—with oil and gas reserves, potential pipeline routes, and a strategic location between Asia's great powers—is a perennial (albeit secondary) prize in the contest for power, influence, and money. The Persian Empire owned much of Afghan territory centuries ago, and swaths of northern and western Afghanistan share a similar language and culture with Iran. According to media reports, Iran maintains extensive ties with the Taliban, Afghan warlords, and opposition politicians. It appears to be cultivating ties to anyone and everyone who might replace the western-oriented Karzai Government. Building a stable and legitimate government in Kabul will be a small step in the larger campaign to limit Tehran's influence.

Russia remains heavily involved in the Central Asian republics. It has worked to oust the United States from the airbase at Manas, Kyrgyzstan. It invests heavily in Tajik border security to counter narco-trafficking. It remains interested in the huge energy reserves in Kazakhstan and Turkmenistan. Russia may be standoffish towards Afghanistan itself, unwilling to repeat the Soviet Union's epic blunder there. But a U.S. withdrawal from Afghanistan followed by Kabul's collapse would likely embolden Russia to assert its influence more aggressively elsewhere in Central Asia or Eastern Europe, especially in the Ukraine.

The Future of NATO

Afghanistan's impact on U.S.-Russia relations raises a related point. In Afghanistan the future of NATO as an Alliance will be written. In 1989 NATO was hailed as the most successful military alliance in history, as even former opponents lined up to join the mutual defense organization. NATO was the institution through which the United States exercised its leadership of the free world and ensured peace in Europe. Every President since Harry Truman has affirmed the centrality of the Atlantic Alliance to U.S. national security. Through NATO the U.S. and its Allies keep the peace in Europe and provide a powerful deterrent to potential rivals, especially Russia. Its continued health and vitality is a vital national security interest of the United States.

Until 2009 NATO was losing the war in Afghanistan and straining at the seams as an Alliance. The NATO-led International Security Assistance Force (ISAF) in Afghanistan is the Alliance's first out-of-area operation in its 60-year history, and it was going poorly until the U.S. troop surge. The Taliban threatened to do what the Red Army could not. Allies have complained that the burden in Afghanistan has been distributed unevenly. Some, like the British, Canadians, and Poles, are fighting a shooting war in Kandahar and Helmand, while others, like the Lithuanians and Germans, are doing peacekeeping in Ghwor and Konduz. The poor command and control—split between four regional centers—left decision-making slow and poorly coordinated for much of the war. ISAF's unclear strategy (the Europeans could not admit for years that ISAF had to fight a "counterinsurgency") was only clarified in 2008 and 2009 when Generals David McKiernan and Stanley McChrystal finally developed a more coherent campaign plan with COIN-appropriate rules of engagement.

A bad end in Afghanistan could have dire consequences for the Alliance. NATO's credibility as a deterrent to Russia is in question. It would not be irrational for a Russian observer of the war in Afghanistan to conclude that if the Alliance cannot make tough decisions, field effective fighting forces, or distribute burdens evenly, it cannot fight a war. If it cannot fight a war, it cannot defend Europe. If NATO cannot defend Europe, the international system is far less stable and more dangerous than at any time since 1945. At the worst, Russia may not stop at Georgia and Ukraine, but directly challenge NATO with an aggressive move in the Baltics. The United States and Europe must prevent that outcome by salvaging a credible outcome in Afghanistan. Afghanistan must be a success to persuade Russia that NATO is still a fighting alliance and to preserve NATO a pillar of U.S. national security.

Transnational Threats

Some critics are unconcerned with hypothetical conventional threats. The Cold War is over, inter-state war is too expensive, and Russian tanks will not make an appearance across the Fulda Gap. Organizing U.S. grand strategy around such scenarios is the perfect example of fighting the last war. NATO is the Maginot Line of our time. These critics highlight new threats that come from asymmetric, non-state actors. In their view, U.S. national security is more threatened by terrorists, insurgency, state failure, ecological disaster, infectious pandemic disease, cyber attacks, transnational crime, piracy, and gangs.

If this view of the world is true, Afghanistan is the epicenter of the new, asymmetric, transnational threats to U.S. and allied national security. It is not terrorists, but drug lords who are the most powerful, armed non-state actors in

Afghanistan. In some years they have controlled wealth equivalent to 50 percent of Afghanistan's GDP and produced in excess of 90 percent of the world's heroin.[5] Their products feed Europe's endemic heroin problem and their wealth has done much to undermine nine years' of work building a new and legitimate government in Kabul. And they will not stop at Afghanistan's borders. In their quest for market share, the drug lords will expand wherever there is demand for their product or potential to grow a secure supply, almost certainly starting in Pakistan, where the trade was centered in the 1980s. Where the drug lords go, state failure and its accompanying chaos and asymmetric threats will follow. The violence and anarchy currently wracking parts of Mexico foreshadow what South Asia's drug lords could bring to Pakistan, India, or even Eastern Europe. Imagine the FATA as a failed narco-state with the profits going to al-Qaida.

South Asia's narcotics-smuggling cartels are dangerously close to seizing control of an entire state and using it to undermine law, order, and stability across and entire region. The poppy and heroin kingpins are fabulously wealthy and powerful, they oppose U.S. interests, undermine U.S. allies, and they are headquartered in Afghanistan. Defeating them is a vital interest of the United States.

Democracy

The United States is in Afghanistan to foster the growth of democracy in the Islamic world. Some will cringe at the very thought of democratization being a part of U.S. foreign policy, so discredited is the idea, for some, by the Iraq war and by neoconservatives' supposed arrogance and stupidity. Others may be generous enough to grant that, despite Iraq, spreading democracy is a nice thing in principle, but relatively unimportant and very hard anyways. Still others will argue that it is even wrong to try because it smacks of utopianism or cultural imperialism.

Fostering democracy around the world is a vital national security interest for a very simple, hard-headed, realist reason.

The democratic peace theory is, broadly, true. Democracies tend not to fight each other. Democracies tend to ally with one another, trade with one another, see the world in similar ways, and settle disputes peacefully. They tend to make more reliable allies, treaty partners, and investment opportunities. They also tend to experience less domestic violence and unrest. Spreading democracy decreases the frequency of war, invests in future allies, and makes America safer.

That does not give the United States license to invade other countries for no other reason than to force them to hold elections (which it has never done, despite caricatures of the Iraq War). And it is true that the process of transitioning to democracy is risky and can temporarily increase the chances of instability, as both Iraq and Afghanistan, among other recent examples, have shown. The democratic peace theory is true among fully democratic countries, ones that have consolidated the institutions and habits of democracy. Many countries have started the process but failed part way because they were unable to manage the social forces unleashed by new freedoms and competitive elections.

But that does not discredit the entire project of democratization. It does mean that U.S. policymakers need to be more careful in how they go about fostering democracy, and they have to take a longer view. Democracies grow on longer timeframes than an electoral cycle or deployment timetable. There is nothing inevitable about the failure of democratization, as realists sometimes seem to imply, just as there is nothing inevitable about its success, as neoconservatives seemed to believe. Democracy has been successfully adapted by nearly three dozen countries outside of Europe and North America. When the United States has the opportunity, as it does in Afghanistan, to choose between encouraging a new democracy genuinely embraced by locals and accepting a tyranny imposed by a minority, the United States should choose the former every time. This is especially true in the Islamic world, where few democracies exist.

Moral Duty

Finally, the United States is involved in Afghanistan to prevent the reemergence of a humanitarian catastrophe. Realists will dismiss this as a legitimate goal of U.S. foreign policy. For those critics, the aforementioned arguments stand alone; one need not agree that the international community has a moral duty to prevent humanitarian catastrophes to recognize our strategic interests in South Asia. On the other end of the spectrum, advocates of liberal interventionism might dismiss our frankly selfish interests in the region. If so, they should recognize that the presence of self-interest does not invalidate the entirely separate threat of humanitarian disaster in Afghanistan.

The danger is real. If Kabul collapses, civil war will almost certainly erupt and the warlords will reestablish their brutal fiefdoms. During Afghanistan's civil wars, from 1992 to 2001, warlords at the head of sectarian militias regularly committed war crimes, crimes against humanity, and ethnic cleansing, as well documented now by the Afghan Independent Human Rights Commission, Human Rights Watch, and the UN. The Taliban amassed a long record of massacring civilians and targeting the Hazara for ethnic-cleansing, notably at Mazar-I Shari in 1998, Robatak Pass in 2000, and Yakaolang in 2001. But their crimes were not unique; Ittihad-I Islami, for example, was accused of ethnic cleansing against the Hazara during a battle in the West Kabul neighborhood of Afshar in 1993. And if the Taliban take power over part or all of Afghanistan, reprisal murders against supporters, even whole tribes, of the Karzai government are likely to be widespread and swift, especially against women and religious minorities.

The international "Responsibility to Protect" (R2P) has been given a new lease on life through the UN's surprisingly bold and energetic response to the civil war in Libya in 2011. It gives the international community the duty to intervene to stop genocide, ethnic cleansing, war crimes, and crimes against humanity, almost all of which the Taliban and many Afghan warlords have a proven track record. Scholars will debate endlessly whether Libya really met the threshold for intervention, but Afghanistan is a much clearer case. If the international community is indeed ready to back R2P with firm action, it should recognize Afghanistan as a prime candidate for sustained intervention.

Stabilization is the Mission

Stabilizing Afghanistan is the only pragmatic policy option that will secure the full range of our interests in South Asia and yield an actual end-point to the war. There are no practical alternatives. Vice President Biden and a growing chorus of others believe the United States should give up rebuilding Afghanistan and, instead, sustain an indefinite worldwide assassination campaign against al-Qaida's senior leaders. This view of the war is myopic, narrow, and troubling. Such a campaign would do nothing to address Pakistan, the drug trade, NATO, the other great powers, or any of our other interests across South Asia. It is also morally troubling—it amounts to a declaration that the United States reserves the right to kill anyone it deems to be a terrorist, anywhere in the world, forever. That would be a dramatic expansion of unaccountable, unchecked power. States should not maintain a state of war indefinitely just because it is too inconvenient to settle the political conditions that led to the war in the first place. War should be the last resort, not the first.

Stabilization and reconstruction operations are not international charity. They are not a superfluous and dispensable exercise in appeasing western guilt, an expensive tribute to humanitarianism, or an act of unvarnished selflessness and goodwill. Stabilization and reconstruction missions are a response to the threat of failed states that threaten regional stability. They are a pragmatic exercise of hard power to protect vital national interests. In the context of Afghanistan, they are the civilian side of counterinsurgency, the primary objective of which is to "foster the development of effective governance by a legitimate government," according to the U.S. Army's Counterinsurgency Field Manual.

Afghanistan's weakness threatens America's security. State failure, chaos, or Taliban rule in Afghanistan will provide a safe haven for al-Qaida, destabilize western Pakistan and endanger its nuclear weapons, become a worldwide headquarters for narcotics traffickers, discredit NATO, invite Iranian and Russian adventurism, and sully self-government and civil liberties in the Muslim world. The international community must stabilize Afghanistan to prevent these catastrophic outcomes.

David Petraeus told Congress in March, when he was still Commander of the International Security Assistance Force in Afghanistan "I am concerned that funding for our State Department and USAID partners will not sufficiently enable them to build on the hard-fought security achievements of our men and women in uniform. *Inadequate resourcing of our civilian partners could, in fact, jeopardize accomplishment of the overall mission,*" (emphasis added).[6] Petraeus could not have been more stark. The United States will lose the war in Afghanistan unless it makes stabilization and reconstruction the overall focus of the mission.

Petraeus was right to be alarmed about the funding levels for the civilians. They are the ones who are acting as embedded advisors to Afghan ministers; helping set up local dispute-resolution councils in provinces and districts; dispensing funds for Afghans to build roads, schools, and hospitals; training Afghans on electric power plant maintenance; and helping cut deals between rival Afghan politicians in Kabul. These things are, in fact, vital war aims because they help create stability in Afghanistan and, thus, South Asia. Under-funding these efforts amounts to trying to kill one's way out of an insurgency, which is both impossible and immoral.

America's Role in the World

America should defeat the Taliban not only to deny safe haven to al-Qaida in Afghanistan but also to preserve stability in Pakistan, contest Russian and Iranian influence, preserve NATO's credibility, fight the global drug trade, promote democracy, and forestall a humanitarian catastrophe. This argument admittedly rests on a prior understanding of America's role in the world. A critic might respond to each of the strategic interests outlined here with a shrug. According to this view, the interests outlined here only peripherally and indirectly affect actual Americans, who are relatively unconcerned with NATO and the global drug trade and think that worrying about Russia is just nostalgia for the Cold War. They might acknowledge that the United States has legitimate disagreements with Iran, but that it should focus on the areas of actual disagreement (nuclear proliferation and terrorism), not engage in a corrupt and suspicious Great Game. Above all, the U.S. has no business promoting democracy in other countries, a foolish and arrogant undertaking.

For example, the signatories of the Afghanistan Study Group opposes the ongoing war in Afghanistan largely because they believe the war is failing and is thus doing more harm than good for America. Balancing against Russian and Iran is a worthy goal, but our military campaign actually makes us weaker, not stronger, by draining our resources and eroding our credibility. Stability in Pakistan is also a good goal, but our military presence in Afghanistan is part of the problem, not the solution, because stationing a huge army in South Asia has provoked the very insurgency the United States is trying to suppress. Democracy is a good thing, but attempting to spread democracy in a poor, non-western country is foolish at best, utopian and hubristic at worst. In this view, U.S. foreign policy should aim narrowly and exclusively at our immediate economic and military needs.

The problem with this brand of realism is that it is short-sighted and its pessimism on Afghanistan is unjustified. The military campaign would weaken the United States vis-à-vis Russia and Iran, and destabilize Pakistan, only if it fails, which is far from certain. Spreading democracy is not charity; it is a strategic investment in future allies. The United States, its allies, and Afghanistan will still emerge stronger at the end of the intervention if it succeeds, which the Study Group and other realists have prejudged to be impossible.

Above all, America's interests are not always best understood narrowly as our immediate economic and military needs, secured through short-term, transactional bargains with other wary powers. Sometimes interests are better framed as longer-term aspirations, towards which policymakers work diligently even if the path ahead is not always clear. Such was the attitude animating U.S. containment policy during the Cold War, when no rational U.S. policymaker could have foreseen or planned the fall of the Soviet Union, but when policymakers were nonetheless nearly unanimous year after year that Soviet expansionism threatened the United States and must be opposed. So too today the path towards peace and stability in South Asia is difficult. The difficulty does not obviate the very real interests that the United States will have in the region for the foreseeable future. And so long as those interests endure, so too should our commitment.

3 JUSTICE AND THE WAR IN AFGHANISTAN

I have argued for more than ten years with friends, family and colleagues that the war in Afghanistan is a just war. My belief in its justice led me to fight in it as a soldier with the U.S. Army in 2002, study the region as an intelligence analyst with the Central Intelligence Agency, and eventually advise two Presidents on its conduct as Director for Afghanistan on the National Security Council. Daily participation in the war effort for a decade reinforced my sense of its justice.

The justice of the war seemed, at least at first, a clear case of self-defense. But simply defending America from another terrorist attack never felt to me like a complete description of what justice would look like for the United States, Afghanistan, or the world after 2001. Fighting al-Qaida and denying safe haven to the group was just, of course. But I felt it was not the entirety of the just cause for which we were fighting. As the years went by, no further terrorist attacks occurred, senior al-Qaida leaders were killed but Afghanistan continued to languish, I felt even more keenly that justice required more than overthrowing the Taliban and getting Osama bin Laden.

But it was not always clear what that broader requirement

of justice was. The argument is complicated by the fact that the ongoing war against the Taliban is sufficiently removed from the terrorist attacks of September 11, 2001 that it is not immediately obvious that the moral calculus involved back then applies today. The initial campaign to overthrow the Taliban, who chose to harbor and protect al-Qaida, was plainly justified self-defense. The Taliban refused to hand over members of al-Qaida and thus became active abettors of the terrorists' aggression. But the present Taliban insurgency started in 2005 and is not self-evidently connected to al-Qaida's ongoing global terrorist campaign: the ongoing war might no longer even qualify as justified self-defense.

The argument is also complicated by the fact that there are at least two distinct just war traditions to which people appeal today. As described by James Turner Johnson in his works and, more recently, by Daniel Bell, there is an older, theological tradition in which right authority to prosecute war flows from God to the state, right intention is the love of one's enemy, and just cause is surprisingly broad. Later, there emerged out of the first tradition a secular, legal tradition in which right authority is the sovereign state, preferably operating within a multilateral coalition; right intention simply proscribes revenge, and just cause is reduced to self-defense. "Just war" means different things to different people depending on which tradition they have in mind.

What does justice require of the American intervention in Afghanistan? Is the ongoing counterinsurgency against the Taliban, as distinct from the initial campaign to overthrow them, just, according to either tradition of just war thinking? If so, does justice require simply the military defeat of the Taliban, or something broader? What would a just outcome look like?

There are three ways of arguing for the justice of the ongoing war in Afghanistan. It can, still, be justified as a war of self-defense. It can be justified as the requirement of *jus post bellum* that we incurred following the initial invasion and overthrow of the Taliban government. And it might be justified by reference to a broader set of causes, including the defense of the oppressed, punishment of the wicked, and restoration of the moral order. Importantly, under any of these criteria the war is about far more than the physical protection of Americans from further terrorist attacks. A just outcome includes as an essential component the reconstruction of Afghanistan and the establishment of some semblance of peace and order there.

Self Defense

The Taliban retains ties to al-Qaida and has consistently refused, even today, to sever its relationship with or denounce the group. If the Taliban retake power in Afghanistan, they will almost certainly invite or tacitly permit al-Qaida or like-minded groups to reestablish a presence in Afghanistan. Preventing that outcome is a legitimate act of self-defense by the United States and its allies. I find this persuasive, but not all foreign policy experts do: some believe al-Qaida has been effectively defeated, others that the Taliban is unlikely to allow the group back into Afghanistan. The truth or falsity of these claims may not be knowable, and is anyway best left to the analysts who study it closely. For our purposes, an important question remains: if (as I do *not* believe is the case) al-Qaida is no longer a threat to the United States, do we have any just cause to remain involved in the war against the Taliban? Are there unmet requirements of justice in Afghanistan?

The most obvious reason to think we have continuing obligations in Afghanistan is because we have made repeated and explicit promises to the Afghans that we will help them defend their country, most recently by designating Afghanistan a Major Non-NATO Ally as part of the U.S.-Afghanistan Strategic Partnership Agreement of 2012. Even if the war is not a war of self-defense by the United States, it most certainly is for the Afghans defending against Taliban aggression— Afghans to whom we have promised of aid and assistance. A cynic might dismiss our promises and alliances as so many rhetorical flourishes that should count for little when we calculate our national interests. The cynics' view is immoral—it is wrong to break our word—but also short sighted. It is foolish to inflict irreparable harm to our credibility by treating our promises so cavalierly. But most importantly, it is a dereliction of the first duty of government to neglect our own security by abandoning allies.

Alliances are a means for states to share the burden of self-defense with others who face a common threat. The strongest alliances merely formalize an existing relationship among states whose security is so intertwined that neither can feel safe without the other. That sometimes requires a state to involve itself in an ally's conflicts even if the threat seems distant. That was true of the United States and Europe in the Second World War. Germany did not attack the United States—Japan did. But American involvement in the European war was plainly just. The Europeans were waging a justified war of self-defense against the Nazis, but lacked the means to win. President Roosevelt understood that the Nazi conquest of Europe was a clear threat to the United States and our way of life. American involvement was a matter of helping others to defend themselves and, thereby, for us to defend ourselves (and this was *before* the United States bound itself to a formal treaty with the European states). The United States, Europe, and the embryonic "United Nations" shared interests so closely that the war against Nazi Germany was a justified war of self-defense: the "self" we were defending included anti-Nazi forces everywhere.

The war against the Taliban is plainly a justified war of self-defense by the Afghans, and it is one which directly concerns American security—not only because of the ties between the Taliban and al-Qaida (which some critics now dismiss), but also because of wide array of interests the United States has across South Asia. These interests include Pakistan's stability and the security of its nuclear weapons, neither of which stand to benefit from a Taliban takeover or a civil war next door; and the transnational drug trade and Iranian regional influence, which are both likely grow if Western forces withdraw in unfavorable circumstances. The United States and Afghanistan share common interests because we face common threats. Our obligation to Afghanistan is thus not (only) a function of charity to an oppressed people, but the requirement of our government to protect ourselves. American aid to Kabul (and Islamabad) is legitimate and justified assistance to the defense of those countries against jihadist groups across the region. The corruption of the Afghan Government, and the autocracy of the Pakistani one, does not deprive them of their right to defend themselves from even worse evils, nor delegitimize our assistance to them: we allied with none other than the Soviet Union to defeat the Nazis.

This broader way of understanding the right of self-defense—to defend our allies and our way of life, not just our territory—points to another, more expansive way in which the war against the Taliban can be described as a war of self-defense. It is a war of collective self-defense by the international community against a global threat. Counterinsurgency expert David Kilcullen has argued that the best way to understand violent Islamist movements such as al-Qaida and its allies is that they are waging a global insurgency against the liberal world order. In this view, whether or not al-Qaida has been defeated is irrelevant: bin Laden's group was only the most famous of a global network of like-minded jihadist terrorist groups and insurgencies that threaten global order. America, as (still) leader of the free world, is justified in helping organize global self-defense against violent Islamists movements anywhere in the world. The Taliban threaten America because they are part of the global jihadist insurgency against the West and the global liberal order we uphold.

That does *not* mean the United States should have a direct combat role against every Islamist insurgency in the world. That would involve American forces fighting not only in Iraq and Afghanistan, but also in Egypt, Saudi Arabia, Chechnya, Malaysia, Indonesia, Somalia, Turkey, Pakistan, and elsewhere. Kilcullen rightly argues that our role should be to "disaggregate" the global insurgency, that is, to sever the links that tie local, provincial movements to the global jihadist movement while bolstering local police and security forces with training and equipment. The tools of a "disaggregation" strategy are diplomacy, law enforcement coordination, border control, disrupting terrorist finance, foreign aid, and security assistance. But a direct American combat role is justified and necessary where the jihadist insurgency threatens to overwhelm local governments or threatens broader regional instability. Afghanistan and Pakistan—al-Qaida's historic headquarters, the location of its senior leadership, supported by the densest network of jihadist groups in the world—is such a place (perhaps the only place).

The idea of global self-defense is admittedly an expansive application of just war doctrine. In typical just war writings, the "self" of "self-defense" is typically a sovereign state or an alliance of states, and they defend against immediate physical harm from conventional threats, like large armies marching across borders—concerns obviously drawn from the early modern era during which many of the classic just war texts were written. But the contemporary security environment is different. States have changed and grown more interdependent thanks to technology, globalization, and a deep network of international institutions. States have allowed themselves to grow interdependent because it serves to underpin a liberal world order from which they benefit and to which they have voluntarily subscribed. And interdependence means that it is easier for a threat against one to translate into a threat against all; some threats are truly global because there is a world order that can be threatened. The terrorist attacks of 2001 killed 28 South Koreans, 41 Indians, and 47 citizens of the Dominican Republic, among thousands of others.

These realities justify a new application of just war thinking, one that recognizes collective self-defense against global threats. Any threat to the liberal world order—including terrorism, piracy, territorial aggression, or proliferation of weapons of mass destruction—is a threat to the states who benefit from that order. Collective action to defend the world order is a form of self-defense. And the United States has a special duty in this context. American policymakers have long recognized that because the United States is the leading power, architect and beneficiary of the liberal world order, America has a unique responsibility to organize global efforts to sustain it.

This is not a call for an American empire: the United States cannot simply provide order unilaterally (if we could, we would be a world government). Nor am I echoing the realists' call to sustain American hegemony for its own sake. It is not *realpolitik* that should drive American policymakers to sustain American hegemony, but moral duty. The liberal world order is just (or, at least, more just than the alternatives), and therefore defending it is a responsibility, whether or not it is in our interest. Of course, it is. We cannot pretend to be a disinterested party—we benefit greatly from the liberal world order—but we should not allow that to become an excuse for inaction or paralysis. A healthy suspicion of our own motives should always lead us to prefer the inconvenient accountability of partners, allies, and coalitions over the seductive ease of unilateralism. But, equally, an awareness of our responsibility should lead us to defend the liberal world order when it is under attack.

Right Intention

A broader understanding of "self-defense" makes clear that the war is not simply about defending Americans from immediate physical harm. We are also helping Afghans defend themselves and their country against unwanted aggression and defending a liberal world order against a global threat. Those require a more expansive understanding of what the war requires and what peace and victory should look like. If we focus exclusively on the first sense of self-defense—protecting the American homeland from attack—we miss the broader requirements of justice and impoverish our view of what we should rightly be trying to accomplish with the use of force.

In particular, we should include the reconstruction of

Afghanistan as an essential goal of the international project there: the ongoing war is an extension of our obligation to rebuild Afghanistan. In the older theological tradition, having right intent meant waging war for the sake of building a more just and lasting peace than that which obtained before the war. As Augustine said (echoing Aristotle, incidentally, a debt rarely acknowledged in the just war literature), "Peace is the end sought for by war. For every man seeks peace by waging war, but no man seeks war by making peace. For even they who intentionally interrupt the peace in which they are living have no hatred of peace, but only wish it changed into a peace that suits them better. They do not, therefore, wish to have no peace, but only one more to their mind." Our war in Afghanistan should culminate with the construction of peace in Afghanistan, not simply the eradication of threats to us.

Daniel Bell in his recent book, *Just War As Christian Discipleship*, expanded this idea in his attempt to revive the theological approach to just war. "If one's intent in waging war is indeed just, if one really loves one's enemies and intends to bring the benefits of peace and justice to them, then one will not abandon them when the shooting stops but will be involved in the restoration of a just peace. If one truly desires justice, then one will stay the course and see justice through to completion," he argued, "which may include a financial commitment, devoting adequate civil affairs and police personnel, as well as perhaps coordinating with nongovernmental organizations in the work of reconstruction." Bell captures this under the heading of right intention, but others have made much the same argument under the heading of *jus post bellum*, of pursuing a just peace in the aftermath of war by fostering reconstruction and by rebuilding local government.[1]

In either case, if we love the Afghans as neighbors, including the Taliban as our enemy neighbor, our war in their country will aim not only at our security, but at their good. The United States overthrew the Afghan government in 2001 and, applying Bell's argument, incurred an obligation to help restore a just peace afterwards. If the initial invasion and overthrow was justified in 2001, then the large post-war reconstruction and stabilization mission in Afghanistan is part of the deal: the international community is obligated to stay and help the Afghans do the positive work of fostering justice and order in their blighted land. To put it another way, if the war is a war of self-defense for the Afghans, and not only Americans, it will aim at peace and justice for Afghans as well as for us.

While this argument may resonant with the faithful, it may offend foreign policy realists who believe that morality should play no role in the conduct of the nation's affairs. That is a separate argument, but in this particular case it is irrelevant because of the nature of insurgency and counterinsurgency warfare. Building governance is an essential part of the counterinsurgency campaign against the Taliban; while it would be a worthy cause by itself, it also happens to be a strategic necessity. The Taliban were able to recoup and launch their insurgency in 2005 because the Afghan government remained weak and efforts to rebuild had been paltry. Seth Jones, an analyst with RAND and the foremost American expert on the Taliban insurgency, has argued that, "Weak governance is a common precondition of insurgencies. The Afghan government was unable to provide basic services to the population; its security forces were too weak to establish law and order; and too few international forces were available to fill the gap. Afghan insurgent groups took advantage of this anarchic situation."[2] Countering an insurgency therefore critically depends on reconstruction and governance reform, on the effort to "foster the development of effective governance by a legitimate government," according to the U.S. Army's counterinsurgency field manual. Reconstruction and stabilization—the requirements of *jus post bellum*—are themselves weapons of war in a counterinsurgency. Our obligation to rebuild Afghanistan and our obligation to defend against the Taliban have effectively merged into a single duty. Realists may disagree with the moral framework in which I have cast this argument, but can agree on the conclusion nonetheless.

The obligation to pursue justice through reconstruction and the restoration of accountable government would stand by itself even absent the Taliban insurgency simply as our obligation to our Afghan allies following the invasion of 2001. Now, however, it has even greater force and urgency because it is a critical part of the ongoing war against the Taliban. This may seem like an odd blurring of lines between *jus ad bellum, jus in bello,* and *jus post bellum,* or between the just cause of self defense and the right intention of fostering peace. But those categories were formulated to structure theological and legal debate and do not always easily map onto very messy cases of real life conflict, especially since the categories largely took shape in the premodern era before the widespread incidence of insurgency and counterinsurgency in the 20th Century. What is plain today is that, at least according to the theological just war tradition, economic reconstruction and governance assistance in Afghanistan is both a moral duty and a crucial wartime necessity.

Humanitarian War

This raises a third and final way in which justice in Afghanistan can be understood, and raises the fraught question of humanitarian intervention. The war in Afghanistan can also be described as a war to punish the wicked and protect the defenseless.

This is the most controversial way to justify a war because it openly legitimizes offensive warfare and the violation of national sovereignty and it rests on a moral judgment against "the wicked." Advocates of humanitarian war hesitate to admit as much, but it is plainly true that wars to stop humanitarian catastrophes are offensive and moralistic in nature. They beg the question: is it just to invade states for their own good? Can we plausibly claim to be working for justice by launching an aggressive war against regimes we claim are wicked and to defend people against their own government?

Surprisingly, despite its controversy, the international

community has taken large steps in this direction in the last fifteen years. Following the worldwide failure to halt the genocide in Rwanda in 1994, the UN and the Government of Canada put together a Commission on Intervention and State Sovereignty to study when, if ever, intervention is justified. The Commission recommended in 2001 that the international community intervene—violate sovereignty—to halt large-scale loss of life and ethnic cleansing (criteria that would be clarified a few years later as applying to genocide, war crimes, crimes against humanity, and ethnic cleansing). The Commission rested its argument on the idea that exercising sovereignty entails a "responsibility to protect" the people under one's care; if a state is unable or unwilling to protect its people, that responsibility passes to the international community. The international community unanimously endorsed this norm at the 2005 World Summit.[3]

Even more surprisingly, these recent developments actually have solid grounding in parts of the just war tradition. The most oft-cited theologians, including Augustine and Aquinas, did not explicitly address the issue (that I have found), probably because they lived in the pre-Westphalian era when sovereignty was a softer concept, when borders were often undefined, and when states did not make a strong distinction between the use of force domestically versus internationally. But the animating principles of the theological tradition—the love of neighbor, the punishment of the wicked—would seem at least to suggest some support for the idea of humanitarian intervention.

The later, secular, legal tradition of just war thought provides almost no support for the idea of a humanitarian war, growing up as it did wholly within the Westphalian order and its strong emphasis on sovereign immunity and territorial inviolability. But in the early modern era, exactly during the transition between the theological and legal traditions, several of the most prominent thinkers who inherited many of the assumptions of the theological tradition but laid the groundwork for modern international law explicitly addressed, and supported, the idea of a humanitarian intervention.

For example, Francisco de Vitoria was a Spanish Catholic writing in the 16th Century about the Spaniards' conquest of the Native Americans in the New World. He wrote broadly against most of the claims the Spaniards made about the justice of their imperial conquest, but he did recognize some legitimate grounds for military intervention. "The tyranny of those who bear rule among the aborigines of America or on the tyrannical laws which work wrong to innocent folk there, such as that which allows the sacrifice of innocent people or the killing in other ways of uncondemned people for cannibalistic purposes," would justify intervention. If the Indians refused to stop, war and regime change should follow: "it is a good ground for making war on them and proceeding against them under the law of war, and, if such sacrilegious rites can not otherwise be stopped, for changing their rulers and creating a new sovereignty over them." Broadly, Vitoria concludes, "punishment can be inflicted for sins against nature," such as cannibalism and human sacrifice.[4]

Similarly, Francisco Suarez, another Spanish Catholic writing a century later, made a nuanced argument in support of intervention on behalf of the oppressed. In his view, a prince may justly go to war in response to an injury against himself or against "any one who has placed himself under the protection of a prince, or even if it be inflicted upon allies or friends." So we may wage war on behalf of others, "But it must be understood that such a circumstance justifies war only on condition that the friend himself would be justified in waging war... a wrong done to another does not give me the right to avenge him, unless he would be justified in avenging himself." This is an important qualification because Suarez wants to draw boundaries around the right of intervention and prevent sovereigns from launching unlimited self-righteous and self-justifying crusades: "the assertion made by some writers, that sovereign kings have the power of avenging injuries done in any part of the world, is entirely false."[5]

Finally, none other than Hugo Grotius himself, father of

international law, follows in Vitoria's and Suarze's footsteps and wrote more extensively on the subject than either. "It is proper also to observe that kings and those who are possessed of sovereign power have a right to exact punishment not only for injuries affecting immediately themselves or their own subjects, but for gross violations of the law of nature and of nations, done to other states and subjects," he wrote. "Upon this principle there can be no hesitation in pronouncing all wars to be just, that are made upon pirates, general robbers, and enemies of the human race." This is so because of "the common tie of one COMMON NATURE, which alone is sufficient to oblige men to assist each other." We are obligated to punish gross wickedness and help the oppressed because of our common humanity. Grotius, like Suarez, places a limit on this obligation: we are not obligated to risk our national survival for others. But barring that exceptional limitation, intervention is justified to stop abnormal tyranny and wickedness. "Where a Busiris, a Phalaris or a Thracian Diomede provoke their people to despair and resistance by unheard of cruelties, having themselves abandoned all the laws of nature, they lose the rights of independent sovereigns, and can no longer claim the privilege of the law of nations." Sovereignty was never designed to shield murderous tyranny, according to Grotius.[6]

Note the these three writers are addressing only exceptional, grievous, abnormal wickedness and harm inflicted upon fellow human beings, like cannibalism, human sacrifice, "unheard of cruelties," "enemies of the human race," and "gross violations of the laws of nature." They seem to be defining a category of acts distinct from normal human sin, from petty injustice, and from the fairly widespread abuse of power found in most states throughout most of history. They recognize that, on rare occasions, some governments fall into exceptional evil, and that is what justifies others in intervening to stop it. That seems to be exactly what the authors of the "Responsibility to Protect" doctrine claim: it has defined four crimes—genocide, war crimes, crimes against humanity, and ethnic cleansing—that are so appalling, so abnormal, as to deprive states of their normal sovereign immunity and territorial inviolability. These are the "gross violations of the law of nature" that we recognize today, and their perpetrators are the "wicked" which the international community has justly agreed to punish. It is moralistic, but if we cannot condemn genocidaires as wicked, we have larger problems.

Afghanistan has seen some of the worst humanitarian suffering and human rights abuses in recent decades. During Afghanistan's civil wars, from 1992 to 2001, warlords at the head of sectarian militias regularly committed war crimes, crimes against humanity, and ethnic cleansing, as well documented now by the Afghan Independent Human Rights Commission, Human Rights Watch, and the UN. The Taliban amassed a long record of massacring civilians and targeting the Hazara for ethnic-cleansing, notably at Mazar-I Shari in 1998, Robatak Pass in 2000, and Yakaolang in 2001. But their crimes were not unique; other militias which are still active today were also guilty of atrocities. Ittihad-I Islami, for example, was accused of ethnic cleansing against the Hazara during a battle in the West Kabul neighborhood of Afshar in 1993.

If the United States withdraws from Afghanistan precipitously, without ensuring a stable government is capable of upholding order, civil war will almost certainly erupt. The warlords who fought the civil wars of the 1990s will reestablish their brutal fiefdoms. The Taliban will take power over part or all of Afghanistan, and reprisal murders against supporters of the Karzai government are likely to be widespread and swift—especially against women, the Hazara, Shia and other religious minorities, and the clans and subclans of Durrani Pashtuns (rivals of the Ghilzai from which much of the Taliban leadership are drawn). The bloodbath and anarchy will make the civil wars in Libya and Syria pale by comparison: it will be one of the great crimes of the 21st Century. Failure to prevent this would be a grave and shameful stain on our national character, akin to the slaughter in Vietnam in 1975.

The United States does not have a moral duty to intervene

everywhere there is injustice: that would entail a global crusade of never-ending conflict worse than the disease it aimed to cure. The "Responsibility to Protect" is rightly limited to exceptional evils. Women, minorities, and political dissidents are oppressed around the world every day, and most of the time the United States is obligated to do exactly nothing. But only most of the time. The gravity of the crime, and our ties to the victims, creates an obligation to intervene. The Taliban's and the warlords' track records of war crimes, and our repeatedly-expressed commitment to the Afghans, suggests the international community, and the United States in particular, bears a responsibility to protect the Afghans from the demons of their recent past. The "Responsibility to Protect" has been given a new lease on life through the UN's surprisingly bold response to the civil war in Libya last year. Scholars will debate endlessly whether Libya really met the threshold for intervention, but Afghanistan is a much clearer case. If the international community is indeed ready to intervene to stop genocide, ethnic cleansing, war crimes, and crimes against humanity, of which the Taliban have a proven track record, it should recognize Afghanistan as a prime candidate for sustained intervention.

Conclusion

In the parable of the Good Samaritan, a traveler on the road to Jericho is waylaid and beaten by thieves. A priest and a Levite pass by the broken and bleeding body before a Samaritan "went to him and bandaged his wounds, pouring on oil and wine. Then he put the man on his own donkey, took him to an inn and took care of him. The next day he took out two silver coins and gave them to the innkeeper. 'Look after him,' he said, 'and when I return, I will reimburse you for any extra expense you may have,'" (Luke 10:34-35). The Samaritan used his own money to care for another on whom harm had fallen.

Afghanistan is the broken and bleeding traveler in our community of nations, having been waylaid and beaten by the

Soviets, the Taliban, and al-Qai'da. Since the Soviet invasion of 1979 Afghanistan has ranked near the bottom of almost every indicator of social, economic, and human development. In 2001 just 13 percent of Afghans had access to safe drinking water. A third or fewer could read or write and less than a million were enrolled in its nearly-defunct schools. Seventy percent were undernourished. The average Afghan lived 46 years; just a third made it to age 65. GDP per capita was among the worst in the world and infant mortality the highest. As *The Economist* rightly summarized in January of 2001, it was the worst country on earth.

The United States has a responsibility to continue the war and to rebuild Afghanistan—to defend ourselves, to rebuild a country whose government we overthrew, and to defend the oppressed. Jesus said that "from everyone who has been given much, much will be demanded; and from the one who has been entrusted with much, much more will be asked," (Luke 12:48). We have emphatically been entrusted with much. Ancient Israel's law code stipulated that "If one of your countrymen becomes poor and is unable to support himself among you, help him as you would an alien or a temporary resident, so he can continue to live among you," (Leviticus 25:35). There is a general Scriptural principle all throughout the Law, Prophets, Gospels, and Epistles that we should *help other people*. Afghanistan is the poor man unable to support himself among the family of nations. Taking of our plenty to help another people in their need is the fulfillment of the Good Samaritan's mandate in international relations.

American security and American ideals rest on a just and lasting peace in Afghanistan. If we intend to protect our lives and preserve our values, there is no substitute for victory. President Bush said in his First Inaugural Address, "I can pledge our nation to a goal: When we see that wounded traveler on the road to Jericho, we will not pass to the other side." The Afghans are wounded and broken and lying on the road; they need our help. We should not pass to the other side.

I wish it were not so. No one has more incentive to "come

home" than the soldier, especially one who has seen his friends and fellows come home maimed or dead. I have lived with this war day in and day out for a decade, and I loath it. As the thousands of soldiers and civilians who have worked for years on Iraq, terrorism, Afghanistan, or Iran know, bearing a burden like this for years on end can be dehumanizing and alienating, especially in the face of a disillusioned public and an ignorant media. General Dwight Eisenhower said it best. "I hate war—as only a soldier who has lived it can, only as one who has seen its brutality, its futility, its stupidity." The only thing that is worse is shirking the claims of justice.

4 FINISH THE JOB

Pessimism abounds in Afghanistan. Violence, NATO casualties, corruption, drug production, and public disapproval in the United States are at record levels. Ahmed Rashid, a prominent Pakistani journalist and an expert on the region, declared the U.S. mission in Afghanistan a failure in his scathing 2008 book, *Descent Into Chaos*. Seth Jones, the leading U.S. scholar on the Taliban insurgency, has argued that the United States had an opening to make a difference in Afghanistan after 2001, but that it "squandered this extraordinary opportunity." U.S. Secretary of Defense Robert Gates attempted to manage expectations when he testified before the Senate Armed Services Committee in January 2009. "If we set ourselves the objective of creating some sort of Central Asian Valhalla over there, we will lose," he argued, "because nobody in the world has that kind of time, patience, and money." U.S. policymakers and the public increasingly doubt that the war can be won. These assessments are based on real and credible concerns about the rising insurgency, the drug trade, endemic corruption, and perennial government weakness.

Yet the stabilization and reconstruction effort in Afghanistan has gone better than is widely believed. The pessimists fail to understand how badly the Afghan state had failed in 2001 and thus are blind to how much it has improved in many areas -- particularly in economic and political reconstruction. The pessimists are right to be worried about the rise of the Taliban insurgency and the weak rule of law, but they also tend to overstate the competence and scale of the insurgency.

Many analysts critical of the war effort have drawn misguided lessons from cartoonish and caricatured versions of Afghan history -- comparing ISAF to the armies of Alexander the Great, William Elphinstone, or Boris Gromov -- to conclude that the laws of history bar foreign militaries from accomplishing anything in the land of the Hindu Kush. They sound dire warnings about U.S. and NATO staying power after a nine-year-old war. But they are wrong on all counts. The insurgency did not pick up steam until late 2005, and ISAF, which started changing its posture and strategy in late 2006, arguably did not implement a coherent counterinsurgency campaign until 2009. It would be myopic and irresponsible to conclude that the international community should walk away from the mission due to a lack of adequate progress.

The greatest threat to long-term success in Afghanistan is not the Taliban, who are fairly weak compared to other insurgent movements around the world. It is the Afghan government's endemic weakness and the international community's failure to address it. Although the international community helped rebuild economic institutions and infrastructure and facilitated elections, it did not invest significantly in government ministries, the justice system, the army and the police, or local governance for the first five years of the intervention, which permitted the Taliban to regroup and challenge the nascent Afghan government.

If additional U.S. and NATO soldiers are matched by a comparable civilian surge, a continuing donor commitment, and a heightened focus on capacity development -- increasing the capabilities and performance of civilian institutions of governance, including the ministries in Kabul, their provincial counterparts, and the legal system -- the international community is likely to achieve its core goals and Afghanistan will have a genuine chance of becoming stable for the first time in a generation. Although serious challenges remain, victory is attainable -- if the troops and their civilian counterparts are given time to complete their mission.

The World's Worst Country

In 2001, Afghanistan was the world's most failed state. The security environment was anarchic, large-scale fighting against the Taliban and al Qaeda continued until March 2002, and following the fall of the Taliban, 50,000-70,000 Northern Alliance militiamen became a poorly managed, largely unaccountable force deployed across the country. There was no professional army or police force, leaving warlords to wage mini wars against one another. The United Nations judged in early 2002 that "banditry continues as a lingering manifestation of the war economy." The drug trade, suppressed during the Taliban's last year in power, sprang back into existence as the poppy crop expanded almost tenfold -- from 20,000 acres to 183,000 acres -- between 2001 and 2002. The resurgence of opium production enriched a new set of elites and created a wealthy criminal class that was neither loyal to Kabul nor cooperative with international forces.[1]

The security environment in 2001 and 2002 was chaotic largely because the Afghan state had ceased to function. The World Bank estimates that in 2000 the Afghan state was in the lowest percentile in all six areas of governance that the bank tracks: voice and accountability, the rule of law, control of corruption, government effectiveness, regulatory quality, and political stability. At that time, the Taliban government collected less than one percent of GDP in revenue, compared to an average of 11 percent across South Asia and 26 percent worldwide. Consequently, the state had an annual budget of merely $27 million -- roughly $1 per person. The Afghan government could not hire skilled workers to run public institutions; in 2001, there were only 1,417 government employees who had graduated from an institution of higher education. And most ministries and the justice sector had effectively ceased to function because they lacked the basic levels of staff, money, and equipment required to do anything. For most practical purposes, such as education, access to clean water, or the protection of property, there was no government.[2]

With an anarchic security situation and a nonfunctional state, the Afghan economy had collapsed by the end of the Taliban's misrule. Afghans were the world's seventh-poorest people in 2001. The International Monetary Fund estimates that in 2002, GDP per capita was about $176 in current U.S. dollars: Afghans lived on about 48 cents per day, comparable to the poorest people in sub-Saharan Africa. Lacking a national currency, different factions issued their own bills for use within their fiefdoms. What little infrastructure the country once had was in ruins: little more than a tenth of the roads were paved, less than one-third of Afghans had access to sanitation, and only a fifth had clean water. Economic collapse led to a generation of lost human capital. A third or less of Afghans could read and write, and only roughly a quarter of school-aged children were enrolled in the country's nearly defunct educational system. In a country of approximately 25 million people, there was just one TV station, eight airplanes, 60 trained pilots, and fewer than 50,000 passenger cars.[3]

The humanitarian situation, in short, was catastrophic. Larry Goodson, professor of Middle East studies at the U.S. Army War College, has estimated that even before the civil war of the 1990s, 50 percent of all Afghans had been killed, wounded, or displaced by the Soviet invasion.[4] There were at least 3.8 million Afghan refugees in neighboring countries and another 1.2 million internally displaced persons in Afghanistan in 2001. Within a year, almost two million refugees and more than 750,000 internally displaced persons had returned to their homes, overwhelming urban areas and creating massive, overcrowded slums.[5] The devastation and neglect took its toll on the Afghan population. Only a third of Afghans survived to age 65. Afghans had the absolute shortest life expectancy and highest infant mortality in the world, according to the World Bank, at 42 years and 165 dead infants per 1,000 live births.[6]

Somalia is often cited as the archetype of a failed state. It is not. Despite Somalia's infamous anarchy, Somalis are still relatively free from government oppression and have not experienced ethnic cleansing or genocide. The Afghans, by contrast, had the worst of all worlds under the Taliban. They had Somalian anarchy, Haitian poverty, Congolese institutions, Balkan fractiousness, and a North Korean-style government. In January 2001, *The Economist* awarded Afghanistan the title of the world's "worst country." Any judgments about the international community's success or failure in Afghanistan need to begin with this benchmark.

A Delicate Constitution

The United Nations set about rebuilding the Afghan state immediately after the fall of the Taliban. Just one day after the liberation of Kabul in November, the Security Council outlined its vision for the next Afghan government. It should be "broad-based, multi-ethnic and fully representative," and "respect the human rights of all Afghan people."[7] The UN, with U.S. help, convened a conference in Bonn, Germany, to select an interim administration and outline a process for reconstruction. The resulting Bonn agreement became a road map for establishing and legitimizing a new Afghan government. The UN endorsed the Bonn agreement, formed and authorized the International Security Assistance Force (ISAF) to help provide security in the capital, and, in March 2002, created the United Nations Assistance Mission in Afghanistan (UNAMA) to coordinate international civilian assistance to Afghanistan.

A principal step in the Bonn process was the drafting and ratification of a new constitution, which UN advisers helped a commission of Afghans draft in 2003. The resulting document protects equal rights for men and women, individual liberty, freedom of expression and association, the right to vote and stand for office, property, and religious freedom. But the document also acknowledges Afghanistan's traditional sources of legitimacy. Article 1 establishes Afghanistan as an "Islamic Republic," Article 2 enshrines Islam as the state religion, Article 3 states that "no law shall contravene the tenets and provisions of the holy religion of Islam in Afghanistan," and Article 62 requires that the president and the two vice presidents of Afghanistan be Muslims. Although the Afghan government's efforts to balance modern law with traditional customs have not always satisfied human rights activists, this constitution is nonetheless an unmitigated improvement over Taliban lawlessness and one of the most progressive constitutions in Central Asia or the Middle East.

The Afghan people's reaction to the constitution was overwhelmingly positive. One member of the *loya jirga* (grand council of elders) convened to ratify the document said after voting for its approval that it was "99 percent based on the will of the people." A group calling itself the National Democratic Front and claiming to represent 47 interest groups endorsed the new constitution, as did a tribal gathering in the borderlands of Paktia Province, illustrating the document's broad base of support among both urban politicos and rural dwellers. Qala-e Naw, a major radio station, rejoiced that Afghans would now enjoy the same rights as the rest of the world.[8]

After the constitution was ratified, the international community funded and administered a voter registration drive and two elections: over eight million Afghans voted in the nation's first-ever presidential contest in October 2004, and 6.4 million voted for the nation's legislature in September 2005 -- Afghanistan's first freely elected legislature since 1973. In 2006, Freedom House upgraded the country to "partly free," and 76 percent of those Afghans surveyed said they were satisfied with democracy, according to the Asia Foundation.[9] Afghans' enthusiastic embrace of voting, representative institutions, and majority rule undermined the arguments of critics who claimed that democracy was an alien transplant doomed to fail in inhospitable Afghan soil. But the success of the Bonn process was not a foregone conclusion. Similar UN-sponsored processes in postconflict countries have collapsed and led to renewed violence, including in Angola and Liberia in the 1990s. It succeeded in Afghanistan because of strong international engagement and support at every stage of the process.

Afghans continue to face challenges in their effort to institutionalize a process of peaceful political competition. The 2009 and 2010 elections were notoriously marred by fraud and low turnout. But it is important to note that power brokers, accustomed to enforcing their writ undemocratically, decided to manipulate the electoral system to serve their own interests rather than ignore it altogether, because they recognized that Afghans now embrace the new democratic constitution as the basis for their state's legitimacy. The international community must pressure the Afghan government to crack down on corruption and develop robust political parties. But to declare total failure is to ignore Afghanistan's political transformation.

Rebuilding Prosperity

In response to the economic and humanitarian emergency in Afghanistan in 2001, the international community undertook one of the largest and most ambitious relief, reconstruction, and development efforts in the world -- eventually committing a total of $22.7 billion in aid to economic reconstruction, economic development, and humanitarian relief between 2001 and 2011.[10] The donors invested heavily in rebuilding the Ministry of Finance, the Central Bank, the Treasury, and the Customs Department and helped phase out the old Afghan currency and launch a new one.

The result was an unheralded and dramatic success. Partly because of U.S. and international aid, Afghanistan experienced a post-Taliban economic boom. Real GDP grew by nearly 29 percent in 2002 alone -- faster than West Germany in 1946 -- and averaged 15 percent annual licit growth from 2001 to 2006, making Afghanistan one of the fastest-growing economies in the world (it was still averaging 13.5 percent through 2009, after a drought in 2008).[11] The pace of its growth was due in part to the low base from which it had started, but the rapid pace itself was an important achievement. Afghanistan had not grown significantly in more than two decades; the economic boom signaled a new era in Afghan life.

Between 2001 and 2009, almost every indicator of human development showed measurable improvement. By late 2008, 80 percent of the population had access to basic health services, up from eight percent in 2001. Also by 2008, Afghan children were being immunized against diphtheria, pertussis, and tetanus (DPT) at the same rate as children in the rest of the world and at a higher rate than in the rest of South Asia. The infant mortality rate fell by a third, and life expectancy inched upward. After the fall of the Taliban, school enrollment skyrocketed from 1.1 million students in 2001 to 7.3 million in 2010 -- almost 40 percent of whom were girls -- promising to double or triple Afghanistan's literacy rate in a decade.

Meanwhile, infrastructure greatly improved with international help. The U.S. Agency for International Development (USAID) built 1,600 miles of roads, and the international community rebuilt three-quarters of the main highway from Herat to Kabul. In total, almost 33 percent of all roads in the country were paved by 2008, up from 13.3 percent in 2001. By 2008, Afghanistan had caught up to its regional and income cohorts in access to telecommunications -- an astonishing feat. The cell-phone industry, nonexistent before 2001, had nearly eight million subscribers by the end of 2008. At the same time, the construction sector tripled in size, donors spent $312 million on water projects, and the number of Afghans with access to an improved water source more than doubled from 21 percent to 48 percent. And access to sanitation rose from 12 percent to perhaps 45 percent.[12]

The impressive growth and improvement since 2001 -- stronger than in any postconflict state in which the UN has deployed a peace-building mission since the end of the Cold War -- demonstrate that progress is achievable with robust resources and international attention. Aid dependency and a poorly diversified economy threaten Afghanistan's long-term economic stability, but the greater risk is that the country's recent progress will unravel unless security is greatly improved.

The UN'S Blind Spot

After 2001, the international community's priority was to prevent the reemergence of the 1992-96 civil war between rival warlords in control of ethnic militias. UN disarmament programs, coupled with the international community's forceful diplomacy, successfully contained fighting among the warlords and prevented the country from relapsing into civil war -- an underrated achievement, especially considering the eruptions of violence during and after other international peace-building missions, such as in Angola in 1992 and 1998, Liberia throughout the 1990s, Cambodia in 1997, and Iraq in 2006-7. The UN secretary-general reported in August 2005 that "factional clashes -- a prominent feature of insecurity three years ago -- have become a localized issue and are no longer a threat to national security."[13]

The international community's strategy in regard to the warlords had a flip side, however. Because the United States and the UN could not confront the warlords directly without risking violence, they had to coax them into giving up their weapons by promising them a place in the new Afghan political order. The warlords thus made a successful entry into Afghan politics as governors, legislators, and cabinet ministers without ever facing prosecution or even a truth commission for alleged war crimes. In hindsight, nearly all scholars and commentators condemn the international community for allowing the warlords to retain power. Yet these same critics often deride the reverse strategy of building up a central government at the expense of local power brokers. After the fall of the Taliban, the international community attempted to navigate between these competing imperatives -- disarming the warlords without unleashing a backlash and building a central government while respecting local authority. The result has been imperfect but better than permitting the warlords to retain their conventional military power, on the one hand, or risking violence by attempting to put them on trial, on the other.

Despite its success against the warlords, the international community failed to train enough new Afghan security forces or successfully contain the residual Taliban threat between 2001 and 2006. Early efforts to train Afghan police and reform the security sector had not achieved notable results by 2006. Washington had spent $4.4 billion on security assistance and had trained 36,000 soldiers and a comparable number of police officers in the first five years -- too few to provide effective security. The police, moreover, were widely reported to be corrupt and incompetent. At the same time, ISAF did not hold large swaths of territory or provide security to the vast majority of Afghans. Indeed, it did not have the mandate or the authorization to do so.

ISAF was relatively small in size, it was initially confined to Kabul, and it was hampered by restrictive rules of engagement and national caveats limiting where the soldiers were permitted to deploy or what kinds of operations they were allowed to engage in. (In 2003, the peacekeeping force had only 5,500 troops assigned to it.) Then, in 2005, ISAF was authorized to operate in the country's northern and western provinces, but it still numbered fewer than 10,000 troops, or four soldiers for every 10,000 Afghans (compared to approximately 42 soldiers per 10,000 civilians in the relatively successful UN-British operation in Sierra Leone in 2002).[14]

The net effect of the international community's light involvement in the security sector, combined with the lack of progress on governance, became evident with the rise of the Taliban insurgency, beginning in 2005. The Taliban and other insurgents had initiated sporadic, uncoordinated attacks against international military forces and the Afghan government in the years following the Taliban's fall from power. Yet they averaged only about four attacks per day nationwide in 2003 and five per day in 2004.[15] In July 2005, Taliban militants assassinated the pro-Western head of the Kandahar Ulema

Shura -- a council of religious scholars -- and then suicide-bombed his funeral, the boldest terrorist attack in the country since 2001. The funeral attack dramatized the Taliban's lethal reach and resilience, the Afghan government's weakness and inability to respond, and ISAF's absence. Following the sudden revelation of the militants' unexpected strength, violence grew markedly worse in the latter half of 2005, increasing to over eight attacks per day and killing 1,268 people. The militants began to make persistent and notable strides in the scope, scale, and sophistication of their attacks. The violence began to escalate dramatically each year thereafter, killing 3,154 people in 2006 and 5,818 in 2007.[16] By late 2005, what had begun as an incoherent and decentralized campaign of violence had gelled into a cohesive insurgency dedicated to eroding Western political will and overthrowing the Afghan government.

The Taliban were able to regroup and launch an insurgency because, effectively, nothing stood in their way. The Afghan government was still unable to offer services or resolve disputes, and there were too few international soldiers to secure the whole country. The state's institutional capacity remained weak, the rule of law was nonexistent, and the security services were still embryonic. "Weak governance is a common precondition of insurgencies," writes Jones, the Afghanistan expert; "Afghan insurgent groups took advantage of this anarchic situation."[17]

Critics are right to argue that the rise of the insurgency is proof that the international state-building campaign had, as of 2006, failed to build a functioning Afghan state. But the intervention did not end in 2006. A U.S. National Security Council review of Afghan policy in late 2006 recognized the emerging challenges and called for substantially more security and development assistance. Following the review, U.S. funding for the Afghan security forces nearly quadrupled, from $1.9 billion in 2006 to $7.4 billion in 2007, and aggregate U.S. spending on security assistance increased fivefold. Starting in late 2007, entire district police units were sent to a training academy, and U.S. trainers were assigned to embed with each unit on graduation. In addition, the international community began experimenting with programs to enlist the aid of local, indigenous, and tribal security forces.

To staff the expanded training programs and provide security while the Afghan forces were coming up to speed, the United States more than quadrupled its military presence in Afghanistan between 2006 and 2010, from 22,100 troops to over 100,000 -- Washington's third-largest military deployment since Vietnam. Partner nations increased their troop deployments as well, from roughly 21,000 at the end of 2006 to 42,381 in June 2011.[18] ISAF deployed nationwide in 2006, assuming responsibility for security assistance in the country's east and south for the first time. General Stanley McChrystal, who was then the commander of ISAF, also began in 2009 to change how U.S. and NATO troops were used. He sought to make the entirety of ISAF a part of the training and mentoring of the Afghan army and police and to focus on protecting the Afghan population. The moves collectively represented a huge shift in emphasis from a "light footprint" counterterrorism mission to a more robust, if still partial, counterinsurgency campaign. As a result, the United States nearly tripled the size of the Afghan army in three years, increasing it from 36,000 soldiers in 2006 to almost 100,000 by the end of 2009. It brought the Afghan police force up to its authorized strength of 82,000 and made incremental progress toward improving its capabilities.

Rising violence and the persistence of a Taliban safe haven in Pakistan have bred pessimism about the war and created a mystique about the resilience of the insurgency. Violence has indeed continued to escalate -- insurgents initiated an average of 19 attacks per day in 2007, almost 30 per day in 2008, and 52 per day from January to August of 2009 -- but the spike in violence is a predictable effect of sending more troops into battle; there are more targets for the insurgents to attack. What matters is not the scale of the violence but the outcome of the battle. While ISAF has made impressive strides in its practice of unconventional warfare, the Taliban have not. The Taliban are not invincible superwarriors hardened by millennia of fighting and xenophobia; indeed, they are hardly even very competent insurgents compared to Nepal's Maoists, Sri Lanka's Tamil Tigers, or Colombia's FARC. They continue to espouse an unpopular extremist ideology and murder large numbers of fellow Pashtun Muslims. Meanwhile, Washington's rumored recent expansion of its drone strikes will erode their safe haven in Pakistan. The single greatest resource the United States now needs is not more troops but more time.

The Governance Vacuum

In one respect, the effort in Afghanistan has seriously faltered. The international community has largely stuck with a failing light-footprint approach toward Afghan governance and capacity development. Partly in reaction to the recent UN missions in Kosovo and East Timor, which were criticized for relying too heavily on experts from abroad, the UN secretary-general publicly and openly instructed UNAMA to "rely on as limited an international presence and on as many Afghan staff as possible."[19] UN officials never considered whether the Afghans, whose human capital had been destroyed by war and depleted by emigration, were able to do the job.

Donors similarly neglected governance programs. They pledged a total of $1.2 billion for Afghan governance and rule-of-law programs between 2001 and 2006, or about $200 million per year, and only disbursed about half that amount. A substantial amount of this was dedicated to the 2004 and 2005 elections, leaving just a few hundred million dollars to train civil servants, judges, prosecutors, and lawyers; rebuild government offices and courthouses; and pay the international advisers and consultants to ministers and other government officials. Considering that Afghanistan was the weakest state in the world in 2001, these funds did not come close to meeting its needs. The international community was effectively asking Afghans with no shoes to lift themselves up by their bootstraps.

For example, a proposed Independent Administrative

Reform and Civil Service Commission was supposed to lead efforts to streamline the bureaucracy, introduce a new pay and grade system, develop merit-based hiring and promotion criteria, and establish a civil service training institute. For this ambitious agenda, the Asian Development Bank gave $2.2 million starting in 2003, and the UN Development Program gave $500,000.[20] A 2007 USAID review of capacity-development efforts in Afghanistan concluded that "capacity building has not been a primary objective of USAID projects" and that "what has occurred has been more ad hoc and 'spotty' rather than systematic and strategic." The review could identify only four ministries out of 25 that were "considered reasonably competent to carry out their primary responsibilities."[21] The Afghan Research and Evaluation Unit, a nongovernmental organization, judged in late 2006 that public-administration reform had been "'cosmetic,' with superficial restructuring of ministries and an emphasis on higher pay rather than fundamental change."[22] The Civil Service Commission did not open until January 2007, and after five years in power, the government could boast of only 7,500 civil servants hired under the new merit-based criteria in a government of 240,000 employees.

Similarly, the international community did not prioritize rebuilding the justice system or improving the rule of law. The U.S. Department of State's Bureau of International Narcotics and Law Enforcement Affairs and USAID did initiate a host of programs, but in practice they were too small to make a measurable difference in the worst justice system in the world. The Afghan government estimated that it would cost $600 million to implement its National Justice Sector Strategy, but donors had disbursed just $38 million in aid to the justice sector by the end of 2006. The UN secretary-general wrote that same year that "with approximately 1,500 judges and 2,000 prosecutors in the judicial system, demand for training far outstrips supply."[23]

As a result of these shortcomings, Afghanistan ranked second worst in the world for the rule of law in 2006, after

Somalia, according to the World Bank's governance indicators. Without the rule of law, corruption predictably exploded as the economy grew. As the political scientist Samuel Huntington noted long ago, modernization without strong institutions almost always yields corruption, and Afghanistan was no exception.

Corruption was increasingly fueled by the drug trade. The poppy crop had soared to 408,000 acres in 2006 and 477,000 in 2007, and Afghanistan was producing 82 percent of the world's poppy and 93 percent of the world's heroin by 2007,[24] making the drug trade worth $4 billion -- equivalent to half of Afghanistan's licit GDP. Because the Afghan government lacked strong institutions and the ability to enforce the rule of law, Afghanistan was becoming a lawless and corrupt narcostate.

When the crisis in governance became apparent with the rise of the Taliban insurgency in 2005 and 2006, the international community moved to bolster its governance programs. In dollar terms, the international community roughly doubled its training efforts in the Afghan civil administration and justice sectors, to $688 million, over the next three years, still a paltry figure relative to Afghanistan's needs. In 2007, USAID started the Capacity Development Program, a $219 million, five-year project to strengthen Afghan institutions such as the Ministries of Finance and Education and the Civil Service Commission.[25] The program was a big improvement but still small in absolute terms. U.S. spending on rule-of-law programs doubled from 2006 to 2007 and nearly doubled again in 2008. The United States also doubled its much more substantial investment in counternarcotics programs -- to $3.3 billion. The increased focus on governance and the rule of law spurred some institutional innovations in the Afghan government, but they have, to date, failed to markedly improve the quality of governance. Afghan President Hamid Karzai named an entirely new slate of justices to the Supreme Court in late 2006. The new court established a Regulation of Judicial Conduct, and the new justices began inspection tours of provincial courts to ensure their compliance with judicial standards. The Afghan government formed an anticorruption unit in the attorney general's office in 2009 to investigate and prosecute cases of high-level corruption, but Afghanistan fell further on Transparency International's Corruption Perceptions Index, to 179th -- second from the bottom -- in 2009. According to a survey conducted by ABC News, the BBC, and the German television station ARD, the number of Afghans who believed the government was doing an excellent or good job fell from 80 percent in 2005 to 49 percent in 2008 -- most likely because their great expectations of 2001 remained unfulfilled.

The international community paid an enormous opportunity cost by failing to play a greater role and provide sufficient resources from the start. Most observers of Afghan governance focus on Karzai's policies, behavior, and fitness for office. But any other Afghan president would face a nearly insurmountable challenge trying to enact policy through an institutional apparatus that, for all intents and purposes, does not function. Others have focused on how centralized or decentralized, institutionalized or tribalized, the Afghan government should be. But that argument is moot. The international community's interest is in making governance effective, whatever it looks like, and that is what the international community failed to invest in building after 2001.

The Road To Victory

The United States is not yet winning the war in Afghanistan, but it is not losing as swiftly or as thoroughly as the current crisis of confidence would suggest. Although Afghanistan remains poor, violent, and poorly governed, it is richer, freer, and safer than it has been in a generation. The security situation is a major challenge, but the United States and its allies have moved since 2006 to adopt a much more aggressive military posture in response -- and with the funding to match it.

The application of increased military resources and a

coherent strategy almost certainly will have an effect on the Afghan battlefield if given enough time to succeed and backed by a complimentary civilian strategy. In particular, U.S. President Barack Obama should show the same flexibility toward his announced July 2011 withdrawal date that he showed toward his initial timeline for withdrawal from Iraq. He wisely announced that the withdrawal will only "begin" in July 2011, leaving open the door for a gradual and phased withdrawal. He should seize on that to give ISAF the time it needs, now that it finally, for the first time in nine years, has adequate resources.

The single greatest strategic threat is the weakness of the Afghan government. Efforts in recent years to increase the size and scope of governance-assistance efforts are a welcome gesture, but they are not enough. The Obama administration should push for a dramatically more ambitious capacity-development program, starting with a much larger civilian presence in the Afghan bureaucracy and court system. Washington should also recognize that it can choose to withdraw from Afghanistan quickly at high risk or slowly at low risk. The programs, budgets, and strategies that are now finally in place have only been operating for a few years; it is unlikely that there will be dramatic progress by July 2011. The Obama administration has calculated that some degree of withdrawal is necessary to pressure the Afghan government, but it should be wary lest a precipitous withdrawal lead to panic in Afghanistan, undoing a decade of careful gains.

If the international community had withdrawn from Afghanistan shortly after the initial round of elections in 2004-5, as it did in Cambodia, Haiti, and Liberia in the 1990s, the intervention would have failed. Governance had not improved, and most important, war had resumed. Remarkably, the international community did not seize on the completion of the Bonn process as a chance to declare victory and withdraw. Reflecting a realism and resilience evident in other recent operations -- such as in Sierra Leone in 2002 and Iraq in 2007 -- international actors recognized the emerging problems and attempted a midcourse correction. They did so in part because prior experiences in Afghanistan had demonstrated that success was possible. The same knowledge should help the United States and its partners overcome the current crisis of confidence.

The Afghan mission is still plagued with difficulties, in particular endemically weak institutions and a poor governance-assistance effort. But recent history has shown that, contrary to popular belief, outsiders can make a positive difference in Afghanistan if given the right time, resources, and leadership.

5 PAKISTAN

The United States has more leverage over Pakistan than is widely appreciated, and it is time for American policymakers to use it. Since 2001 two successive administrations have tried to persuade Pakistan to end its support for militants, including the Afghan Taliban and the Haqqani network, exclusively through aid, diplomacy, and persuasion with few sanctions or conditions—an approach of all carrots and no sticks. They did so in the belief that Pakistan's fundamental problem was a lack of capacity, not will.

They were wrong. Elements of the Pakistani state are willfully complicit in actions directly harmful to U.S. interests in South Asia, according to a wide and consistent body of reporting. Pakistan is able to aid militants with impunity because it pays no cost in terms of American support or aid. The solution therefore is not to give Pakistan more aid or improve public diplomacy, but to use a mix of aid, conditions, and sanctions to change Pakistani officials' cost-benefit calculus about its support for militants. The United States must make cooperation with militants more costly than cooperation with the US.

Kerry-Lugar

Recent history illustrates how difficult it is to calibrate a tougher approach with Pakistan. In 2009 the Obama administration made a small move in this direction when it tried to shift the emphasis in the U.S.-Pakistani relationship from one primarily focused on military affairs to one focused on a broader range of issues, including democracy, civilian rule, and trade, in addition to stability—but simultaneously built more explicit conditions into the relationship. The Enhanced Partnership with Pakistan Act (the Kerry-Lugar Bill), as the cornerstone of the new approach, offered to triple economic assistance to Pakistan from 2009 through 2014 so long as Pakistan made progress towards a series of benchmarks on governance and security.

The Kerry-Lugar Bill was controversial in Pakistan because of the conditions the U.S. Congress rightly built into it. The full amount of aid under Kerry-Lugar ($1.5 billion per year) is only available if the U.S. Secretary of State certifies annually that U.S. aid to Pakistan is contributing to the "consolidation of democratic institutions," supporting the "expansion of the rule of law" and "respect for internationally-recognized human rights," and promoting "economic freedom and sustainable economic development."[1] Similarly, in order to continue providing military aid to Pakistan, the Secretary of State must certify that Pakistan "has demonstrated a sustained commitment to and is making significant efforts towards combating terrorist groups," specifically by "ceasing support, including by any elements within the Pakistan military or its intelligence agency, to extremist and terrorist groups," and preventing them "from operating in the territory of Pakistan."[2] Additionally, military aid is strictly conditional on the continuance of civilian rule in Pakistan.

Pakistani military and civilian officials expressed outrage at the condition placed on the new economic assistance. They felt the conditions were condescending and tantamount to an infringement on their sovereignty.[3] The Pakistani Army issued a rare statement expressing "serious concern" about the bill and reiterating that "Pakistan is a sovereign state."[4] The Obama administration's attempt improve U.S.-Pakistan, bolster the civilian government, and nudge Pakistan towards more responsible behavior appears to have backfired.

Worth the Risk?

The Obama administration's error may have been its hesitance to risk a complete falling-out with Pakistan. Placing conditions on Pakistan while professing continuing friendship served neither purpose; it only succeeded in angering Pakistani politicians without compelling different behavior from them. What the United States has not attempted yet is a single-minded focus on changing Pakistan's behavior, whether that entails friendly or unfriendly relations and whether it requires aid or coercion.

A tougher approach will, of course, risk losing the few benefits the United States derives from its partnership with Islamabad, notably intelligence cooperation. But a harder line is unlikely to lead to a collapse of the Pakistani state, the failure of civilian government, or its takeover by jihadists. The dangers to Pakistan, and the importance of U.S. aid, have been exaggerated. The state is not in danger of immediate collapse, U.S. aid is not crucial to its survival, and the Pakistani Taliban has no prospects of defeating the Pakistani Army.

Bruce Riedel, a veteran Pakistan expert who spent 30 years studying the region with the Central Intelligence Agency and developing U.S. policy towards Pakistan on the National Security Council staff, calls a jihadist Pakistan the "nightmare scenario" and goes so far as to sketch scenarios of how it might come about. He nonetheless admits the prospect "is neither imminent nor inevitable."[5] Similarly, scholar Anatol Lieven judges that there is "not remotely enough" support for Islamist extremism "to revolutionize Pakistan as a whole,"[6] a judgment shared by other Pakistan experts like Stephen P. Cohen, who argues that the view of Pakistan as "a center of Islamic revolutionary activity…is not accurate."[7] The peaceful Islamist parties have never performed well in Pakistani elections and were most recently voted out of office in Khyber Pakhtunkhwa Province in 2008. Their militant counterparts are no stronger: the Pakistani Taliban have virtually no prospect of overrunning the Pakistani Army, one of the largest in the world, or seizing Islamabad by force. They can only make progress in the time-honored fashion of insurgents everywhere: by offering a more compelling vision of governance than the state offers, something that the Taliban on both sides of the border have markedly failed to do year after year. Meanwhile, the Pakistani Army has made notable strides in its counterinsurgency efforts since 2008 and violence in the tribal areas has declined over the past year.[8] The Pakistani Army does not lack the will, motivation, or capacity in its fight against the Pakistani Taliban, which means the presence or absence of American aid, alliance, and support is not important enough to determine the outcome of that conflict.

America has real and vital national security interests at stake in South Asia, most of which are endangered by Pakistan's decades-long policy of supporting and tolerating militant groups. If indeed it is time to get tough with Pakistan, what would that look like? There are at least six major options: reduce aid; cut trade ties; rescind Pakistan's status as a major Non-NATO ally; end intelligence cooperation; designate individuals, organizations, or the Pakistani state a sponsor of terrorism; and initiate or expand unilateral US operations in Pakistan. Each option has advantages and disadvantages, but it is time to take them more seriously as options available to pressure Pakistan. These options could be imposed as a series of escalating punitive measures until Pakistan shows a demonstrable commitment to ending support for militants.

Aid Conditionality

The first step Washington could take is to reduce economic or military assistance to Pakistan. Pakistan is the 10th largest recipient of aid in U.S. history, having received more than $52 billion since 1950.[9] Indeed, compared to the other top recipients of U.S. aid, Pakistan has received aid more consistently over the last six decades time than any other country. The other top recipients typically received aid in concentrated pockets of time, such as the large tranches of aid Britain and France received after World War II or that South Korea and South Vietnam received during the U.S. wars there. Contrary to the Pakistani narrative that Washington is a fickle ally, the United States has been a remarkably consistent funnel of money, interrupted only by temporary halts after 1965 and 1990. Since the terrorist attacks of 2001, the United States provided $7.4 billion in civilian assistance to Pakistan,[10] and that number is set to double over the next several years under the the Kerry-Lugar Bill. Similarly, the U.S. provided $14.6 billion in military aid to Pakistan from 2002 to 2011.[11]

It is too early to pass definitive judgment on Pakistan's progress against the Kerry-Lugar metrics. But the trend lines are not encouraging and none of the conditions have been persuasively met. Pakistan ranked 134th on Transparency International's Corruption Perceptions Index in 2011, down from 79th in 2001. Rampant networks of corruption and nepotism do not undermine the Pakistani state; they *are* the state. Journalist and scholar Anatol Lieven wrote last year that the state of the rule of law in Pakistan "calls into question the whole project of creating a unified modern state."[12] As for Pakistan's support to militants, Admiral Michael Mullen, the U.S. Chairman of the Joint Chiefs of Staff, told Congress in public testimony last September that "the Haqqani network acts as a veritable arm of Pakistan's Inter-Services Intelligence agency."[13] Few doubt that several major militant groups, including the Afghan Taliban, continue to "operate in the territory of Pakistan," in violation of the language of the Kerry-Lugar bill. Finally, even civilian rule is questionable: despite Asif Zardari's election as a civilian Prime Minister in 2008, it is unclear if he exercises effective control over Pakistan's foreign and defense policy.

More importantly, the goals of the Kerry-Lugar bill may simply be too ambitious. It is not within the United States' power to reengineer Pakistan's political culture, build its economy, or implant the rule of law. At a time when most observers are beginning to doubt the ability of the U.S. to effect meaningful change in Afghanistan, a much smaller, poorer country to which the U.S. has given vastly larger sums of money, it seems unreasonable to expect that the much smaller amount of aid given to Pakistan will make a substantial difference there. U.S. aid is unlikely to be the deciding factor in Pakistan's future.

Given these realities, the United States could easily invoke the conditions in the Kerry-Lugar bill to reduce or eliminate economic and military assistance to Pakistan to signal its displeasure for Pakistan's continuing support for militants. The Obama administration has already taken half-hearted steps in this direction, suspending $800 million in Coalition Support Funds last year after Pakistan expelled U.S. trainers in retaliation for the raid on Osama bin Laden's compound in Abbottabad.[14] And the U.S. Congress threatened to cut $33 million in aid after Pakistan jailed the doctor who allegedly helped locate bin Laden.[15] The Secretary of State is empowered to issue a national security waiver for most of the Kerry-Lugar conditions, but it is unclear why any American administration would want to do so. Unless or until Pakistan verifiably ceases support to militant groups hostile to American interests (not just those who attack the Pakistani state) and makes demonstrable progress against them, the United States has no discernible interest in providing it aid.

U.S.-Pakistan Trade Ties

Similarly, the United States could reduce or close off the growing economic ties between itself and Pakistan. While not related to the Kerry-Lugar legislation directly, U.S.-Pakistan trade ties have been growing quickly over the past decade, and Pakistan needs the United States as a trading partner far more than the United States needs Pakistan. Helped by the signing of a U.S.-Pakistan Trade and Investment Agreement in 2003, trade between the United States and Pakistan more than doubled from $2.8 billion in 2001 to $5.8 billion in 2011. While insignificant to the gigantic American market, the trade relationship represents a meaningful portion of Pakistan's $200 billion economy and was Pakistan's top destination for exports in 2010 (by comparison, Pakistan is the United States' 57th largest trading partner). Additionally, Pakistani workers in the United States contribute a sizeable portion of the $8.7 billion in remittances to Pakistan from abroad. And U.S. businesses account for $517 million of foreign direct investment in Pakistan, almost one-quarter of the total.[16]

The U.S. has options available to it to slow or reverse these growing trade ties, whether by pulling out of the 2003 agreement, finding a complaint to file against Pakistani trade practices, or imposing import duties to offset Pakistan's relatively more lax environmental and labor practices, for example. This kind of coercive economic diplomacy would be unlikely to hurt any important American interest because of the small U.S. economic interests at stake in Pakistan, but would disproportionately hurt Pakistani business interests, many of whom are influential in Pakistan's elite, patronage-driven political system.

Critics may complain that this move (or cutting off economic assistance) would hurt the very factions within Pakistan that the United States should be doing the most to support—civilians, businessmen, and entrepreneurs, as opposed to the military and Islamist factions. That criticism is unpersuasive on three counts. First, it exaggerates the importance of civilians and moderates in Pakistan's political system, who, after all, failed to reduce Pakistan's support for militants while in power either during the 1990s or since 2008. Secondly, it presumes the United States has the ability to manipulate the balance of power among Pakistan's factions to its advantage; nothing in recent history suggests the U.S. foreign policy apparatus possesses that ability. Thirdly, this view also exaggerates the distinction between civilian moderates on the one hand and military autocrats on the other. In fact, the military prospers in part with and through its partnership with big industrial interests, with whom it is deeply enmeshed. Economic coercion against Pakistani trade interests may hit the Pakistani Army in the pocketbook, where it hurts the most.

Major Non-NATO Ally (MNNA) Status

Another step the United States could take against Pakistan is to formally dissolve the U.S.-Pakistan "alliance." The origins of the U.S.-Pakistan alliance is often said to be a pair of treaties signed in 1954-55: the Southeast Asia Treaty Organization (SEATO) and the Central Treaty Organization (CENTO), both of which tied the signatories together in a NATO-like mutual defense pact. Pakistani officials themselves often invoke this history to remind American counterparts that Pakistan has been the United States' "most allied ally" in the world. Such assertions are false: Pakistan withdrew from SEATO in 1972 and CENTO in 1979. The United States bears no formal treaty obligation towards Pakistan, and has borne none in more than 30 years.

The contemporary U.S.-Pakistan alliance is of much more recent vintage. In 2004, President George W. Bush designated Pakistan a Major Non-NATO Ally (MNNA). The MNNA designation was created by Congress in 1989 as a way of identifying America's major strategic partners without the burdensome requirements of a formal treaty. It confers a range of benefits, including participation in U.S. Defense Department research and development projects, preferential access to U.S. military surplus supplies, the use of U.S. loans to finance weapons purchases, and expedited applications for space technology exports.[17] More importantly, the designation has a powerful symbolic value: it is a public affirmation of a country's affiliation with the United States, a global badge of American approval. Although the designation does not technically carry a security guarantee or legally obligate the United States to come to the defense of a designee, the label of "ally" implies as much. Only 14 states and Taiwan have been given the MNNA status. Pakistan was the most recent, along with Morocco and Kuwait, in 2004.

The designation is a public symbol of the United States' continuing belief in Pakistan's fidelity as an ally. And the alliance has paid some benefits for the United States. As Pakistani officials are the first to point out, Pakistan has been a generally reliable and helpful ally in the hunt for members of al-Qaida. With the exception of the raid against Osama bin Laden, Pakistani security forces have been a part of operations against many of the senior al-Qaida leadership found in Pakistan, including Khaled Sheikh Mohammad.[18] The Pakistani government is also reported to have privately allowed the U.S. to carry out the rumored drone strikes against militants in Pakistan, despite its public denunciation of them.[19] And thousands of Pakistani soldiers have been killed fighting against the Pakistani Taliban.

But Pakistan's cooperation against al-Qaida and the Pakistani Taliban is, of course, in its own interest, as both groups have targeted the Pakistani state. The true worth of an ally is its willingness to cooperate in matters of peripheral concern, or even to change its definition of interest for the sake of its ally. The war in Afghanistan admittedly put Pakistan in a difficult position, forcing it to choose between the United States and the Taliban clients it had fostered and encouraged since 1994, and many Pakistani officials understandably believe they have an interest in maintaining both relationships. But just because their predicament is understandable does not mean the United States should tolerate it. If American policymakers conclude, reasonably, that Pakistan has failed to behave as an ally in the war against the Afghan Taliban or the Haqqani Network, who are the groups most directly responsible for the ongoing fighting in Afghanistan and the deaths of American soldiers, the United States should rescind the MNNA designation and dissolve the U.S.-Pakistan alliance. So long as Pakistan prioritizes the Taliban over the United States, the U.S. has little reason to treat the former as an ally while fighting a war against the latter.

The move would trigger some diplomatic consequences.

Stripping Pakistan of its status as a MNNA would be a highly-visible and public way of signaling that the United States no longer considers Pakistan an ally. By ending what Pakistanis consider to be a nearly 70-year-old alliance, it would compel Islamabad to rethink its grand strategy and probably increase its ties with China (although it is unlikely Beijing will be able to offer the same level of aid or the same quality of training and equipment that the U.S. gives to Pakistan). But dissolving the alliance is unlikely to threaten Pakistan's continued operations against al-Qaida. With or without the U.S. alliance, al-Qaida has already given Pakistan ample reason to go after the group because of its role supporting and sponsoring domestic terrorism against Islamabad.

Intelligence Cooperation

Another option available to U.S. policymakers is to draw down or end the United States' long-standing intelligence cooperation with Pakistan. Washington and Islamabad have had a long intelligence liaison relationship which has benefited Pakistan and goes back to the early days of the Cold War. According to Riedel, the CIA veteran, Pakistan allowed the United States to use its territory for intelligence collection in the 1960s, including an air base for aerial reconnaissance of the Soviet Union and technical facilities to intercept communications.[20] The U.S. Air Force U2 reconnaissance aircraft that was shot down over the Soviet Union in May 1960 had taken off from an air strip in Pakistan. The cooperative relationship between the two states' intelligence agencies flowed from the newly-formed alliance and was part of what Pakistani officials understood to be their duty as members of CENTO and SEATO in exchange for America's security guarantee.

U.S.-Pakistani intelligence cooperation, like all aspects of the U.S.-Pakistan relationship, cooled following the 1965 war but revived in the 1980s during the Soviet-Afghan War. As is well known, the United States and Pakistan, among others, cooperated closely, including with their respective intelligence assets, to fund and arm the Afghan mujahedin in their war against the Soviet Union. Following the withdrawal of the Soviet Union and the imposition of sanctions on Pakistan for its nuclear-weapons development, such close ties cooled again.

A similar arrangement with new facilities almost certainly started again after 2001, although details are unavailable or speculative in unclassified sources. Pakistan has cooperated with the United States against al-Qaida and other militants, principally through its law enforcement forces and Directorate C of the ISI, its counter-terrorism branch.[21] Pakistan probably shares selected bits of intelligence it gleans about al-Qaida with American military forces and intelligence agencies, and, as noted above, it reportedly has given its private consent to the U.S. drone campaign, possibly including air strips inside Pakistan for drone operations.

Pakistan benefits from this relationship. The United States gives Pakistan a substantial amount of military assistance in the form on money, equipment, and training, some of which probably extends to or includes intelligence activities. Additionally, intelligence relationships are typically two-way: the United States probably shares some of its intelligence with Pakistan in exchange for the information Pakistan offers to the U.S. Finally, the U.S. has, on occasion, directly targeted Pakistan's enemies in the course of its drone campaign, including a reportedly successful strike against Pakistani Taliban leader Baitullah Mehsud in August 2009 and an apparently unsuccessful one against his successor, Hakimullah Mehsud, in January 2012.[22]

Reducing or eliminating intelligence cooperation with Pakistan would deprive Pakistan of these benefits, but would also, of course, hurt the United States' own intelligence operations in the region. However, none of the losses stemming from ending the intelligence relationship would be irreplaceable. Washington's close relationship with Kabul and its growing ties with New Delhi suggest that the United States has alternatives for basing key facilities and sharing intelligence in South Asia. Afghanistan, for example, would be just as good a location for basing assets to conduct reconnaissance and surveillance of militant networks in South Asia, and a superior one for basing assets oriented towards Russia and Iran. Additionally, since whatever information Pakistan shares with the United States comes at Pakistan's discretion, it is unclear how useful the information is: surely no information is shared that Pakistani officials believe could be used to hurt their own interests or, presumably, their militant proxies. In other words, losing the intelligence Pakistan shares with the United States is probably not a great loss. Finally, refocusing the drone campaign to focus exclusively on groups that target the United States rather than those who are fighting Pakistan is simply a more economical use of resources. Helping Pakistan fight the Pakistani Taliban might be good diplomacy, but it has not thus far helped win the war against the Afghan Taliban—and it might have the unintended consequence of breeding complacency in the Pakistani Army about the strength and resilience against their homegrown militants.

Terrorist Designations

A more serious step the United States could take would be to designate Pakistan, or specific Pakistani actors, as sponsors of terrorism. There are several tiers of designations available to U.S. policymakers.

First, the Secretary of Treasury could designate individual Pakistanis as Specially Designated Nationals (SDNs) for complicity in terrorism or drug trafficking, freezing their assets and prohibiting Americans from doing business with them. For example, Hamid Gul, a retired Pakistani Army officer who headed Pakistan's Inter-Services Intelligence (ISI) from 1987 to 1989 and was architect of Pakistan's strategy of using militant proxies against India in Kashmir, is almost universally reported to have retained ties to militants, including the Taliban. He is reportedly on the U.S. terrorist watchlist and American officials submitted his name to the United Nations to be included on the list of international terrorists,[23] but the Treasury Department has not yet sanctioned him. Sanctioning Gul by name, and other retired and active Pakistani Army officers like him, may not have many material consequences unless Gul already has ties to American businesses. But, importantly, it would communicate to Pakistani officials that employment by the Pakistani state does not give them immunity for links to terrorists. It would impose a cost on Pakistan for its use of proxies and refuse to grant the thin cover of deniability such proxies supposedly give them.

Secondly, the U.S. Secretary of State could designate Directorate S of Pakistan's Inter-Services Intelligence as a Foreign Terrorist Organization (FTO). Several U.S. Congressmen and Senators have urged the Secretary for several years to designate Iran's Islamic Revolutionary Guard Corps Qods Force (IRGC-QF) an FTO for its role in training and equipping Hezbollah and militants in Iraq and Afghanistan.[24] Directorate S of the ISI, in charge of external operations, plays a similar role as the IRGC-QF.[25] The ISI was the principle instrument by which Pakistan funded, trained, equipped, and in some cases created the Afghan mujahedin resistance groups in the 1980s, from which it naturally evolved to play the same role for Kashmiri insurgent groups in the 1990s and the Taliban after 1994, all of which would have fallen under the jurisdiction of Directorate S.[26] If the Haqqani Network is a "veritable arm of the ISI," as Admiral Mullen claimed, Directorate S is the shoulder. An FTO designation makes it a federal crime to provide material support to the group, bars members from entering or staying in the United States, and obligates U.S. financial institutions to freeze any of the group's funds it hold. It also "stigmatizes and isolates" the group in the eyes of the international community.[27] This step would end any remaining U.S. ties with Pakistani intelligence.

Designating Directorate S of the ISI as an FTO would only be possible if the U.S. argued that it was a rogue organization outside the control of the Pakistani state. That may or may not be a plausible position to take, but its truth is less relevant than the political implications of it. U.S. policymakers may feel compelled to argue (or pretend) that Directorate S is rogue because if it is not, the necessary and logical next step is to designate Pakistan a state sponsor of terrorism. This final tier of terrorist designation would end all forms of U.S. assistance to Pakistan and trigger a wide range of sanctions and export controls. Currently there are four officially-designated state-sponsors of terrorism (Cuba, Iran, Sudan, and Syria), all of whom are treated as pariahs in the international community in part because of their links to terrorism (as well as their regular violations of human rights and, in some cases, proliferation of weapons of mass destruction). This step would go beyond merely dissolving the U.S.-Pakistan alliance and would instead begin to treat Pakistan as a hostile power.

Unilateral U.S. Operations in Pakistan

Finally, as a last resort, the U.S. could initiate or accelerate unilateral operations in Pakistan, including drone strikes and ground incursions, and including operations in Quetta. Details of U.S. operations in Pakistan are hazy and uncorroborated for obvious reasons, but the reporting in public sources has been fairly consistent. The United States flies unmanned aerial vehicles (UAVs) over Pakistan to conduct intelligence, surveillance, and reconnaissance of terrorists and militants, remotely piloted by U.S. drone operators located elsewhere. Some of these drones are armed and, since 2004, the drones have launched about 300 attacks on militant targets inside Pakistan, killing between 1,782 and 2,768 people, about 17 percent of whom were civilians, according to the most comprehensive publicly-available study done on the drone program to date. The targets of the drone attacks were primarily Taliban fighters but also included al-Qaida, Haqqani Network, and other militants. The strikes take place exclusively in the Federally Administered Tribal Areas, heavily concentrated in North and South Waziristan.[28] In addition to aerial attacks, the United States has launched limited ground attacks by U.S. military personnel inside Pakistan, including a failed raid against militants in Angor Adda in September 2008 and the successful raid in Abbottabad against Osama bin

Ladan in May 2011.[29]

Pakistani officials have condemned the ground incursions, may soon demand the end of the drone program, and may have already shut down a base used for drone maintenance and repair last fall.[30] But instead of winding the program down, the United States might explore the opposite option. If the drone program is, as President Obama publicly claimed in January, a useful means of launching pinpoint strikes against America's enemies while minimizing the violation of another country's sovereignty,[31] then the United States ought to develop a way of expanding the scope and scale of the program without Pakistan's consent or complicity.

Specifically, the U.S. might expand the geographic range of drone strikes. Several top al-Qaida leaders, including Osama bin Laden and Khaled Sheikh Mohammad, were found hiding in major urban centers well outside the Federally Administered Tribal Areas. The Taliban senior leadership is widely believed to be headquartered in Quetta, Baluchistan Province, 500 kilometers south of the FATA and beyond the current drone program's reach. Aside from the Pakistani government's predictable resistance to drone strikes in urban areas, precise targeting in a compact urban environment rather than the more wide-open rural environment of the FATA would clearly be difficult. But the potential payoff should at least prompt U.S. officials to explore the option seriously.

Additionally, as a last resort, the United States could expand the target set at which such operations are aimed, to include current and former Pakistani military and intelligence officials complicit with militants. Such a policy could be interpreted as an act of war against Pakistan, triggering far reaching and undesirable consequences, including reprisals by Pakistan or its proxies against American targets. The only justification for such a drastic step would be a finding by the President that Pakistan's support for militants has long-since constituted an act of war against the United States.

Cart Before the Horse?

A critic may respond that these policy options make no strategic sense because maintaining friendly ties with Islamabad is more important than defeating militant Islamist groups. Cracking down on Pakistan for the sake of defeating the Afghan Taliban may win the battle of Kabul, but lose the war for South Asia by driving Pakistan into open hostility. According to this view, Pakistan is vastly more important than Afghanistan by dint of its sheer size, its nuclear weapons, its role in the Muslim world, and its much bigger and more viable economy. The U.S. should continue to engage Pakistan, give it more economic assistance, and encourage the growth of civilian rule—essentially the Obama administration's strategy. In this view, if the United States has to take a loss in Afghanistan to preserve good ties with Pakistan, that is an acceptable price to pay.

The obvious rejoinder is: what good ties are left to preserve? Pakistan is already in virtual open hostility to the United States. The United States has received precious few benefits for its aid, alliance, and complicity with Pakistan over the past decade. Pakistan is, indeed, more important and powerful than Afghanistan, but that simply means it is all the more important to have a coherent, credible policy towards it, not that the United States should never offend it. China is also a powerful state, but that does not mean the United States is obliged to pretend it is an ally or offer it billions in aid. The United States is paying a high and rising cost for its current strategy towards Pakistan. American soldiers are dying at the hands of militants encouraged by Islamabad. Terrorists planning attacks against the United States and its allies operate in Pakistan almost unbothered by the Pakistani government. Pakistan's rivalry with India could trigger nuclear war with global radiological fallout. Pretending Pakistan is an ally and giving it money has prevented none of these developments.

Nor is the United States likely to succeed if its policy depends on changing Pakistan's political culture to be more respectful of civilian rule. Whatever civilian allies the United

States may have inside the Pakistani government have failed to appreciably change the direction of Pakistan's foreign policy. And, as I argued above, there is little in recent history to suggest that the U.S. foreign policy apparatus has the ability to change this dynamic. The fabled civilian moderates either do not exist or they are powerless, in which case they are not allies for whom it is worth sacrificing American lives.

Finally, the outcome of the conflict in Afghanistan is not immaterial to U.S.-Pakistani relations, as if the United States could simply walk away from Kabul as a gesture of goodwill to Islamabad. Losing in Afghanistan would actually hurt U.S. interests in Pakistan, not help: taking a loss there would mean civil war or a Taliban victory in Kabul, which in turn would empower Pakistani militants, give them a safe haven, and put even more pressure on Islamabad to co-opt or appease them. Winning in Afghanistan, by contrast, would put further pressure on militants in Pakistan and demonstrate the United States' commitment to building a lasting stability in South Asia in which militancy has no part. Pakistan may be the horse drawing the Afghan cart, but you don't spend time grooming the horse if the cart is on fire.

Conclusion

Any one of these policy options carries with it risks and downsides for the United States. Pakistan is sure to respond in some fashion, but it is unclear what critics fear Pakistan would do that it has not already done. The list of possible reprisals—sponsor terrorism, proliferate weapons of mass destruction, meddle unhelpfully in Afghanistan, threaten India—is simply the recent history of Pakistani foreign policy. Furthermore, some U.S. options, like cutting off aid to Pakistan, would actually benefit the United States by saving it money in a time of fiscal austerity. Some options may push Pakistan closer to China or reduce a small amount of U.S. trade overseas, but those are small consequences compared to the ongoing harm inflicted on the United States by militant groups that Pakistan supports or tolerates. Others, such as cutting off intelligence cooperation or expanding unilateral operations, carry more serious consequences and should held in reserve against a more serious deterioration in the U.S.-Pakistan relationship in the future.

American policymakers should not initiate every one of these policies simultaneously, and hopefully will never need to impose most of them. Rather, the United States should recognize that its current policy towards Pakistan—free cash, a formal alliance, and a blind eye towards Islamabad's failings and betrayals—has simply failed to secure vital American interests in South Asia. Pakistan is actively working to oppose American goals in Afghanistan; it has been one of the greatest proliferators of weapons of mass destruction in recent history; it supports a range of militants and terrorists; and its policy towards India is increasingly of American concern in light of the growing U.S.-Indian ties of the past two decades. In light of these enduring features of Pakistani foreign policy, a reappraisal of U.S. policy towards Pakistan is long overdue.

6 AFTER 2014

The United States is not scheduled to withdraw from Afghanistan in 2014, contrary to widespread misreporting by media outlets. President Obama made clear in his May 2012 speech in Afghanistan in that the United States will continue to train Afghan security forces and undertake counter-terrorism operations—which are likely to require at least 20,000 to 25,000 U.S. troops operating in Afghanistan for years to come. 2014 is a date for transition, not withdrawal: the international community has pledged to hand over leadership for security to the Afghan government—no more, no less. Afghan leadership will come with a heavy helping hand from the continued presence of international partners.

Nor is that unwise, considering what is at stake for U.S. interests across South Asia. The war in Afghanistan has lasted far longer and been more difficult than anyone anticipated at the outset, but that does not obviate the very real interests that involved the United States there in the first place—denying safe haven to al Qaida and its affiliates—nor other interests crucially affected by the outcome of the war. These interests include Pakistan's stability and the security of its nuclear weapons, neither of which stand to benefit from a Taliban takeover or a civil war next door; the transnational drug trade and Iranian regional influence, which are both likely grow if Western forces withdraw in unfavorable circumstances; and humanitarian considerations, as the bloodbath in a collapsing Afghanistan is likely to dwarf the recent civil wars in Libya and Syria.

None of the worst outcomes are inevitable, and international forces still have the opportunity to shape a least-bad outcome. Two decisions will be particularly important. First is the size and mission of the post-transition international military force. While President Obama rightly pledged U.S. assistance to training Afghan security forces and continuing counter-terrorism operations, he gave no indication that U.S. forces will continue to support the Afghan Army's counterinsurgency efforts—for example, by sustaining the Village Stability Operations (VSO) that have contributed to significant military progress over the last few years. Keeping a slightly larger post-2014 force—perhaps 35,000 U.S. troops instead of 25,000—to sustain counterinsurgency support would increase the likelihood that the Afghans will capitalize on ISAF's recent gains and drive the Taliban to the negotiating table.

The second major decision is the level and type of governance assistance the United States and international community give to Afghanistan. Governance assistance, the long-neglected pillar of the international project, is crucial for enhancing capacity and fighting the corruption that has undermined years of statebuilding efforts. A relatively small investment of several thousand personnel from Army Civil Affairs and the Civilian Response Corps as embedded trainers and advisors throughout the Afghan state at all levels could dramatically change the trajectory of Afghan governance and, thus, the war. American policymakers face a series of decisions over the next 18 months that collectively may be more determinative for the future of Afghanistan and the region than the previous 11 years put together. Despite the reluctance of either presidential candidate to talk about Afghanistan, the war is not over; in fact, it is only now entering its culminating phase, and American interests in South Asia hang in the balance.

Proving Progress is Possible

In 2009 the International Security Assistance Force (ISAF) and its Afghan partners finally began making progress against the Taliban insurgency, in large part because they began to shift tactics to address the challenges of Afghanistan's rural insurgency. While U.S. commanders had long talked about applying counterinsurgency doctrine in Afghanistan, they were hampered by their experience fighting a very different war in Iraq. The Iraqi insurgency was primarily urban, in response to which U.S. forces were able to spread out across Baghdad and other major cities in 2007 and 2008 and still retain a relatively high concentration of troops, making the application of counterinsurgency there relatively more straightforward and less logistically demanding. By contrast, the Afghan insurgency is primarily rural. The Taliban operate across a huge region, from Konar in the northeast within sight of the Pamir Mountains to Nimruz in the far southwestern desert bordering Iran—far larger than Iraq's Sunni triangle. The result is a war that is far more dispersed than the Baghdad-centric war in Iraq, presenting a different operational environment and different tactical challenge for U.S. forces.

After several false starts, in late 2009 ISAF under General Stanely McChrystal was finally able to adapt counterinsurgency doctrine to the rural context of Afghanistan through the Village Stability Operation (VSO) program. VSO, which bears some resemblance to the Combined Action Program (CAP) used Vietnam, is "a bottom-up stability program that embraces the vital role rural villages play" in Afghanistan, according to the U.S. Special Operations Command's summary of the program. It involves U.S. Special Forces "moving out of their forward operating bases and into Afghan villages," so that the Americans were better postured to "identify…grievances and sources of instability." Once there, the Special Forces "were able to address the local grievances of many Afghans by re-empowering local, tribal institutions of security, economic development, and governance."

In other words, U.S. troops live in rural Afghan villages to form relationships with tribal elders. Once there, Special Forces help train Afghan Local Police (ALP), essentially local defense forces, and help connect these new security forces to local governance structures. The goal is to "stabilize the environment by helping local nationals stand up for themselves."[1] VSO is both the application of classic counterinsurgency doctrine and an adaptation to the unique requirements of the Afghan context. One scholar judged that "VSO may be the last best hope for stabilizing Afghanistan."[2] Some concerns remain over vetting and oversight, but the Defense Department judged in April that "Overall security has improved in most villages as a result of VSO [and] governance activity is generally higher than throughout the rest of Afghanistan," a judgment the UN broadly shared. The program is not manpower-intensive: only 5,200 special operations forces were assigned to the program in April, but had trained over 13,000 ALP in about 100 villages.[3]

Backed by the surge of U.S. troops ordered by President Obama, the added resources and new tactics showed demonstrable progress against the Taliban insurgency. Last fall the Department of Defense announced that violence in Afghanistan finally began to decline in 2011—the first time it has done so in at least five years.[4] Importantly, the military's good news was corroborated by credible, third-party observers. Several months prior to the Defense Department's report, the UN Secretary General noted in his periodic report to the Security Council that "The number of districts under insurgent control has decreased...As a result of the increased tempo of security operations in northern and western provinces, an increasing number of anti-Government elements are seeking to join local reintegration programmes."[5] The same month, the New York Times—hardly a mouthpiece for military propaganda—reported that "The Taliban have been under stress since American forces doubled their presence in southern Afghanistan." It went on to report that "the Afghan Taliban are showing signs of increasing strain after a number of killings, arrests and internal disputes that have reached them even in their haven in Pakistan." The killings "have unnerved many in the Taliban and have spread a climate of paranoia and distrust within the insurgent movement."[6] Both the U.S. Department of Defense and the UN reported that violence continued to decline in the spring of 2012 compared to the same time period in 2011.[7]

Consolidating Security Gains

The surge of U.S. troops and their adaptation of counterinsurgency doctrine demonstrated that progress against the Taliban insurgency is possible. The question now is how to sustain progress as security operations are increasingly led by Afghan forces and as international forces transition to a supporting role over the next year and a half. The UN-authorized International Security Assistance Force (ISAF) is scheduled to wind down by the end of 2014, but President Obama has already successfully worked with European allies to ensure an enduring international military presence beyond that. At the very least, it will include continued training for the Afghan army and police. In 2010 NATO agreed at its summit in Lisbon to invest in an "enduring partnership" with Afghanistan and pledged that its involvement would "endure beyond ISAF's current mission."[8] At the NATO Summit in Chicago earlier this year, ISAF's Declaration on Afghanistan was even more explicit, promising NATO support to Afghanistan "up to 2014 and beyond," and promised to establish "a new training, advising and assistance mission."[9]

Additionally, the U.S will keep a counter-terrorism capability in Afghanistan for the foreseeable future. The U.S. retained a counter-terrorism force in Afghanistan separate from, or only loosely connected to, ISAF over the years; it is difficult to envision the U.S. withdrawing the capability under any circumstances. In the new U.S.-Afghan Strategic Partnership Agreement, signed in May 2012, Afghanistan agreed to "provide U.S. forces continued access to and use of Afghan facilities through 2014, and beyond as may be agreed...for the purposes of combating al-Qaeda and its affiliates."[10]

These two missions—counter-terrorism and training Afghan forces—will require a significant military deployment that will probably be larger than any other deployment of U.S. troops in the world outside of Europe and East Asia. David Barno, who commanded U.S. forces in Afghanistan from 2003 to 2005, recently estimated that the counter-terrorism mission alone would require 10,000 troops.[11] The two missions together could easily require more than 20,000 – 25,000 troops to remain in Afghanistan. Because media outlets regularly report 2014 as a "withdrawal" deadline instead of a transition deadline, it will take Americans by surprise that this is already U.S. policy. In the absence of any decisions to the contrary, bureaucratic inertia will leave tens of thousands of U.S. troops in Afghanistan well beyond 2014.

However, it is unclear if the narrow counter-terrorism and training missions would be sufficient to secure U.S. interests in Afghanistan. While the Afghan army and police are increasingly capable, counterinsurgency is a difficult skill that requires tight civilian-military coordination at local and national levels. Almost 15,000 U.S. troops have been withdrawn from Afghanistan over the last year. The Defense Department warned that, despite the gradual fall in violence, "The insurgency remains a resilient and determined enemy and will likely attempt to regain lost ground and influence." It accurately predicted the Taliban would continue its campaign of "assassinations, intimidation, [and] high-profile attacks." Particularly troubling, according to the UN, has been the Taliban's campaign of "targeted assassinations of influential political and religious leaders" in southern provinces.[12] The Taliban are counter-attacking against ISAF's focus on bolstering local governance.

The U.S. need not sustain its current role as the lead element in the counterinsurgency campaign against the Taliban (although it may be prudent to slow the transition if circumstances warrant), but it can continue to provide support to the Afghans. In particular, the VSO program is a highly effective component of joint Afghan-international counterinsurgency efforts and does not require a high level of international manpower. Barno estimated that adding a "substantial U.S. advisory presence [and] significant U.S. enablers" (similar in concept to the VSO program) to the counter-terrorism and training missions would bring the total U.S. troop presence to about 35,000 (accounting for both advisers and trainers as well as the logistics, supply, and quick-reaction forces needed to support them).[13] President Obama's transition plan already will require up to 25,000 troops. Sustaining VSO operations after 2014 at a cost of only 5,000 to 10,000 additional U.S. troops would go a long way towards consolidating the security gains of recent years and mitigating the risk that the Taliban would use the transition as an opportunity to retake the initiative and attempt to overwhelm outlying rural areas.

Statebuilding: the Missing Ingredient

Securing a few rural villages and killing more *talibs* will not stabilize Afghanistan, however. The essential condition for victory is, and has always been, the construction of a state capable of governing Afghanistan. As President Obama has been at pains to stress, this is not "nation-building." It is the simple requirement of counter-insurgency, the primary objective of which is to "foster the development of effective governance by a legitimate government," according to the U.S. Army counterinsurgency manual. International officials regularly and publicly acknowledge the link between governance and security. For example, At Lisbon, NATO urged the Afghans to "improve governance, deliver basic services, and promote licit economic activity," and crack down on corruption in order to "translate security gains into political gains." In other words, counter-insurgency is competitive statebuilding; Kabul must out-govern the Taliban to demonstrate to the population why it deserves their support. Only when the international community can be confident that an effective government will enforce its writ throughout Afghanistan can it safely withdraw the props of support it has provided to Kabul for 11 years.

Which makes all the more alarming the lack of progress on governance in Afghanistan. The Afghan government has ranked almost dead last on Transparency International's Corruptions Perceptions Index every year since 2007. Its scores on political rights and civil liberties by Freedom House have actually declined since 2008. The World Bank, which rates all states in the world according to six indicators of governance—voice and accountability, political stability, governance effectiveness, regulatory quality, control of corruption, and the rule of law—continues to rank Afghanistan among the very worst in the world in all categories. The Defense Department reported earlier this year that "Setbacks in governance and development continue to slow the reinforcement of security gains and threaten the legitimacy and long-term viability of the Afghan Government." After 11 years, the Afghan government is still one of the weakest and least capable states on the planet.[14]

The international community bears part of the blame for its failure to invest greater resources in governance assistance. While the United States has committed almost $80 billion in aid to Afghanistan since 2001, two-thirds has gone towards training the Afghan army and police, according to the Special Inspector General for Afghanistan Reconstruction (SIGAR).[15] Only an average of $2 billion per year has gone towards "governance and development," of which the bulk has gone towards high-price economic development projects, like the refurbishment of Kajaki Dam in Helmand Province or the restoration of Highway 1, rather than comparatively more mundane efforts to train civil servants, judges, and prosecutors. What little money has been available for governance assistance has been consumed by expensive elections and voter registration efforts in 2004-5 and 2009-10. Despite the widespread acknowledgement that Afghanistan needed massive help, and despite the massive sums of money that flowed into the country over the last decade, the Afghan state—its ministries, courts, and regulatory agencies—has received an ironically tiny amount of help.

One key consequence of the low level of resources devoted to governance assistance has been the lack of sustained international civilian engagement with Afghan counterparts. In 2001 the UN Secretary General openly instructed the UN Assistance Mission in Afghanistan to "rely on as limited an international presence and on as many Afghan staff as possible…thereby leaving a light expatriate 'footprint.'"[16] The U.S. Embassy had fewer than 300 personnel assigned to it in late 2008—a fraction of the size of the embassy in Baghdad. Afghans frequently complained that diplomats and contractors were posted to Afghanistan for only short periods of time, sometimes only three months at a stretch. Without the ability to invest in human relationships, the international community could do little to improve Afghanistan's human capital or create a network of transparency and accountability in Afghan ministries.

General David Petraeus told Congress in March 2011, when he was Commander of the International Security Assistance Force, that "I am concerned that funding for our State Department and USAID partners will not sufficiently enable them to build on the hard-fought security achievements of our men and women in uniform. Inadequate resourcing of our civilian partners could, in fact, jeopardize accomplishment of the overall mission."[17] Petraeus' remarkable statement—that the United States could lose the war in Afghanistan without greater funding for civilian reconstruction and governance assistance—has largely fallen on deaf ears. U.S. aid for governance and development declined by almost $1.5 billion— one-third of the total—from 2010 to 2011, and continued to decline in 2012. This is especially worrisome considering that the World Bank and Afghan Central Bank recently judged Afghanistan will require $4 billion in assistance per year for ongoing reconstruction efforts.[18]

A New Approach

In response to the dire governance situation, the Afghan government and its international partners created the Civilian Technical Assistance Program (CTAP) in 2010. Under CTAP, Afghan ministries identify specific needs and ask for international technical experts to help meet them. Donor nations identify experts—usually government employees or contractors—and embed them in the Afghan government. The technical experts are not intended to solve the Afghans' problems, but to teach them how to solve it themselves. "The main role for Technical Assistance is not to do the job of the government for it, but to build skills, improve systems and reform structures and processes. Technical Assistance should be based on the principle 'give a man a fish, and you feed him for a day- teach a man to fish, and you feed him for his whole life,'" according to the program's website.[19] CTAP civilians are expected to commit for two years, and they focus especially on establishing standard bureaucratic operation procedures, reengineering business processes, restructuring organizations, and building skills in the Afghan workforce. CTAP is intended to be demand-driven, response to the Afghans' identified needs (rather than donors' whims), and fully transparent and accountable.

CTAP treads a sensitive line because it involves international personnel operating in the Afghan government. That is why the program stresses Afghan ownership. Technical assistance is only initiated at the Afghans' request, and the international technical experts are limited to training and advising, not executing Afghan government policy. Those safeguards are important lest CTAP become a Trojan Horse for a de facto UN trusteeship, like those that governed Kosovo and East Timor. Erecting an international authority inside the Afghan government without Afghan consent would be dramatically counterproductive. These dangers are unlikely, however, because the international community has as little appetite to take over Afghanistan as the Afghans have for allowing it. On balance, CTAP holds great promise to redress the failings of international governance assistance efforts.

The U.S. government has two tools almost custom-designed for exactly the sort of work identified by the CTAP: Army Civil Affairs and the Civilian Response Corps (CRC). The U.S. Army's Civil Affairs branch exists to interact with civilians in a military theater. This includes "military operations that help to stabilize or to continue the operations of the governing body or civil structure of a foreign country," according to the Army's Civil Affairs field manual. One of the five core tasks of Civil Affairs is "support to civil administration," and Civil Affairs develop expertise in six functional areas: rule of law, economic stability, governance, public health and welfare, infrastructure, and public education and information. Civil Affairs operations "may include performance by military forces of activities and functions normally the responsibility of local, regional, or national government." This is not a new capability: it was Civil Affairs teams (under a different name) that fanned out across West Germany after World War II first to govern the occupation zone, then to partner with vetted anti-Nazi Germans to rebuild their institutions of government. Civil Affairs soldiers bring "cultural awareness, training in military-to-host nation (HN) advisory activities, and civilian professional skills that parallel common government functions," to the U.S.'s foreign policy tool kit. (Their status as military personnel should not be a barrier to their participation in the Civilian Technical Assistance Program. As special operations forces, Civil Affairs soldiers can be exempt from normal military requirements, such as the wear of the uniform).

The CRC, overseen by the State Department's Bureau of Conflict and Stabilization Operations, is the civilian counterpart to Army Civil Affairs. It was founded after 2004 in response to the widespread recognition that the United States needed an institutionalized civilian capability to respond to post-conflict situations. The CRC is "is a group of civilian federal employees who are specially trained and equipped to deploy rapidly to provide conflict prevention and stabilization assistance to countries in crisis or emerging from conflict," according to its website. They are civilian reservists available to be called up and deployed to fragile states to assist with peacebuilding efforts. Among their core capabilities are the "establishment and monitoring of good governance programs," "providing expertise and monitoring in good economic governance," and "providing technical expertise on basic services such as clean water, electricity, sanitation, communication, and other basic services,"—all skills the CTAP seeks to employ within the Afghan government.

The relevance of Civil Affairs and the CRC to Afghanistan's governance needs, and specifically to the CTAP, should be clear. The Afghan state needs advice and training, identified and vetted through the CTAP, from international technical experts. The United States has the human resources, institutionalized and trained in Civil Affairs and the CRC, to do exactly that. The Afghans should be aggressive about their CTAP requests and push the international community to finally put programs, personnel and budgets behind the lofty rhetoric of the past decade. The international community, starting with the United States, should be equally aggressive in their willingness to deploy hundreds, even thousands, of technical experts to meet Afghanistan's governance needs. Improving the capacity of the Afghan state could be the true game-changer for which the international community has been searching for a decade. In particular, greater technical capacity will enable the Afghan government to provide the infrastructure, legal environment, and regulatory framework for its private sector to exploit the $1 trillion of natural resources, including iron, copper, gold, and lithium, reportedly buried under Afghanistan's mountains—creating jobs and expanding the tax base in the process.[20] When it comes to governance assistance, it is time to put up or shut up.

The concept of deploying technical experts to Afghanistan is neither far-fetched nor prohibitively expensive. U.S. military personnel have acted as embedded trainers and advisors in the Ministries of Defense and Interior for years, and various contractors and aid agencies have embedded personnel the civilian ministries. These efforts, however, were often ad hoc, tiny, uncoordinated with Afghan-identified needs, and limited by short tours. In 2009 President Obama called for a civilian surge and succeeded in increasing the U.S. Embassy's roster from 300 to 1,200 people. Again, the new personnel were not matched to specific needs in the Afghan government. In addition, they deployed at the very height of the war, limiting their ability to travel and work outside large, fortified compounds. The improving security situation makes it safer for more technical experts to be deployed further outside the wire, into provinces and rural areas, while the withdrawal of tens of thousands of combat forces will generate more than enough cost savings to pay for a few thousand technical experts. In all, a true surge of technical experts will not appreciable increase the financial burden on the United States—but it could change the trajectory of Afghan governance and mean the difference between state failure and stability.

Finally, investing in face-to-face ties with Afghan officials at all levels of government might finally give the international community the relationship capital to persuade the Afghans to adopt a series of political reforms that observers have long argued are necessary for the long-term health of Afghanistan's political system. These reforms include devolving more power to provinces and localities, making governors and district chiefs elected rather than appointed, harmonizing the electoral calendar, and reforming the electoral law to abolish the single non-transferable vote system, all of which will make the Afghan state more flexible, responsive, and accountable.

Conclusion

A great deal of emphasis has been placed on reconciliation negotiations with the Taliban in recent years—rightly so, as negotiations are a normal and necessary part of ending an insurgency. Barring, on the one hand, a catastrophic withdrawal by the international community (which would open the way for a Taliban victory), or, on the other, a complete about-face by Pakistan (which would lead to the Taliban's final defeat), the war is likely to end with a negotiated ceasefire and political settlement. The U.S. and the international community should continue to pursue talks and accept reconciliation with anyone who severs ties to al-Qaida and pledges to abide by Afghan laws. Encouraging the formation of a non-violent Taliban political party would be a helpful step in this direction.

But negotiations are not a silver bullet that will end the war and secure U.S. interests in South Asia at a stroke. The shape of the final agreement matters a great deal. A verifiable agreement by the Taliban to end militant activity and separate from al-Qaida could be the best and most cost effective opportunity to secure our interests in South Asia, including denying safe haven to al-Qaida, reversing the momentum of the Pakistani Taliban insurgency, and denying Iran a proxy in Kabul. But an agreement without safeguards or enforcement mechanisms could be the excuse the U.S. invokes to justify abandoning the region as its collapses. Getting the details right requires sustaining both political and military pressure on the Taliban. Killing *talibs* on the field of battle while out-governing them on the streets will change the cost-benefit calculation of joining or supporting the insurgency. If death is likely and Kabul is doing its job, only last-stand die-hards will cling to a broken and inept movement. In other words, a robust peace agreement is the effect, not the cause, of coherent strategy.

Such an outcome is possible. The dream of a peaceful, democratic, modern, and prosperous Afghanistan, if it ever was realistic, is out of reach thanks to a decade of missteps and missed opportunities. But the opposite scenario—unending war, al-Qaida's return, mass refugee flows, bumper poppy crops, encroaching Iranian influence—is not inevitable. The international community has real options that are fiscally and politically feasible to consolidate recent progress and lay the groundwork for lasting stability, which is all the United States needs to protect its most vital interests. The rest will be up to the Afghans.

ABOUT THE AUTHOR

Dr. Paul D. Miller is an Assistant Professor of International Security Studies at the National Defense University in Washington, D.C. He previously served as Director for Afghanistan on the National Security Council staff from September 2007 to September 2009. He supported the 2008 and 2009 Afghanistan-Pakistan strategy reviews for the Bush and Obama Administrations. He served as a political analyst for the Central Intelligence Agency specializing in South Asia prior to his work in the White House. He also serves as an officer in the U.S. Army Reserve and was deployed to Afghanistan in 2002.

Miller holds a PhD from Georgetown University in International Relations and a Masters in Public Policy from Harvard University. His writing has appeared in *Foreign Affairs*, *Survival*, *The National Interest*, the *World Affairs Journal*, *PRISM*, *Studies in Intelligence*, the *Washington Post*, the *Weekly Standard*, *Books and Culture*, *The City*, and he has forthcoming articles in *First Things* and *Small Wars and Insurgencies*. He blogs on foreign policy at ForeignPolicy.com's <u>Shadow Government</u>, and on literature and film at <u>Schaeffer's Ghost</u>. His research interests include state failure and statebuilding, reconstruction and stabilization operations, South Asia, intelligence and foreign policy, and U.S. national security process.

Dr. Miller is a member of the American Political Science Association, Veterans of Foreign Wars, and the Council on Foreign Relations (Term Member). Dr. Miller lives in Cheverly, MD, with his wife and two children.

NOTES

Chapter 1

[1] Measured as a percentage of GDP. Stephen Daggett, "Costs of Major U.S. Wars," Congressional Research Service, June 29, 2010.
http://www.fas.org/sgp/crs/natsec/RS22926.pdf
[2] My analysis of data from Office of Management and Budget, *Historical Tables*.
http://www.whitehouse.gov/sites/default/files/omb/budget/fy2012/assets/hist.pdf
[3] Thomas Barfield, *Afghanistan: A Cultural and Political History* (Princeton University Press, 2010), pg. 66.

Chapter 2

[1] Gallup. http://www.gallup.com/poll/116233/Afghanistan.aspx
[2] *A New Way Forward: Rethinking U.S. Strategy in Afghanistan*, The Afghanistan Study Group, 2010.
http://www.afghanistanstudygroup.org/NewWayForward_report.pdf
[3] *Pakistan Index: Tracking Variables of Reconstruction and Security*, The Brookings Institution, December 29, 2011.
http://www.brookings.edu/~/media/Programs/foreign%20policy/pakistan%20index/index20111229.PDF
[4] Liam Stack, "Pakistani Taliban helped Faisal Shahzad, it's not on US list of terrorists?" *Christian Science Monitor*, June 23, 2010.
http://www.csmonitor.com/World/terrorism-security/2010/0623/Pakistani-Taliban-helped-Faisal-Shahzad-it-s-not-on-US-list-of-terrorists
[5] *Afghanistan Opium Survey 2011*, UNODC, December 2011.
http://www.unodc.org/documents/crop-monitoring/Afghanistan/Afghanistan_opium_survey_2011_web.pdf
[6] "Full Text of General Petraeus' testimony to Congress," March 15, 2011.
http://www.longwarjournal.org/threat-matrix/archives/2011/03/full_text_of_general_petraeus.php

Chapter 3

[1] Daniel Bell, *Just War as Christian Discipleship*, Brazos Press, 2009.
[2] Seth G. Jones, "The Rise of Afghanistan's Insurgency: State Failure and Jihad," *International Security* 32, no. 4 (Spring 2008, 2008): 7-40.
[3] *The Responsibility to Protect*, The International Commission on Intervention and State Sovereignty, December 2001. Available at http://responsibilitytoprotect.org/ICISS%20Report.pdf. United Nations

General Assembly Resolution, "2005 World Summit Outcome,"
A/RES/60/1, 24 October 2005. Gareth Evans and Mohamed Sahnoun,
"The Responsibility to Protect," *Foreign Affairs*, Vol. 81, No. 6, Nov/Dec
2002, pp. 99-110.
[4] Francisco de Vitoria, *De Indis De Jure Belli* (1532), First Relectio,
Section 3, Paragraph 15. Available at
http://en.wikisource.org/wiki/De_Indis_De_Jure_Belli/Part_2
[5] Francisco Suarez, *Three Theological Virtues: On Charity* (1621),
disputation 13, Section IV, paragraph 3. From *War and Christian Ethics,*
2ⁿᵈ Edition, Arthur F. Holmes, ed. (Baker Academic, 2005), pg. 206-7.
[6] Hugo Grotius, *On the Law of War and Peace* (1625), Book II, Chapter
20, "On Punishments," and Chapter 25, "The Causes of Undertaking War
for Others." Available at http://www.constitution.org/gro/djbp_220.htm
and http://www.constitution.org/gro/djbp_225.htm .

Chapter 4

[1] Anthony H. Cordesman, *The Afghan-Pakistan War: Developments in
NATO/ISAF and US Forces* (Washington, D.C.: Center for Strategic and
International Studies,[2009]). Michael Bhatia, Kevin Lanigan and Philip
Wilkinson, *Minimal Investments, Minimal Results: The Failure of Security
Policy in Afghanistan* (Kabul, Afghanistan: Afghan Research and
Evaluation Unit,[2004]). Report of the Secretary General of the United
Nations on the Situation in Afghanistan, March 18, 2002. UNODC,
*Afghanistan Opium Survey - Oct 2002*United Nations Office on Drugs and
Crime,[2002])
[2] Central Statistics Organization, *Afghanistan Statistical Yearbook 2003*;
Daniel Kaufmann, Aart Kraay and Massimo Mastruzzi, *Governance
Matters VIII: Aggregate and Individual Governance Indicators, 1996-
2008*, 2009)
[3] Central Statistics Organization, *Afghanistan Statistical Yearbook 2003*
(Kabul: Central Statistics Organization, Islamic Republic of Afghanistan,
2003).International Monetary Fund, *Afghanistan: Selected Issues and
Statistical Appendix* (Washington, D.C.: ,[2005]).; International Monetary
Fund, *Islamic Republic of Afghanistan: Selected Issues and Statistical
Appendix* (Washington, D.C.: International Monetary Fund,[2008]).;
International Monetary Fund, *Islamic Republic of Afghanistan: Fifth
Review Under the Three-Year Arrangement Under the Poverty Reduction
and Growth Facility* (Washington, D.C.: International Monetary
Fund,[2009]).; Cramer and Goodhand, *Try again, Fail again, Fail Better?*
131-156; 7.

[4] Larry P. Goodson, *Afghanistan's Endless War : State Failure, Regional Politics, and the Rise of the Taliban* (Seattle: University of Washington Press, 2001).

[5] UNHCR, *Statistical Yearbook 2001* (New York: United Nations High Commissioner for Refugees, 2002).; UNHCR, *Statistical Yearbook 2002* (New York: United Nations High Commissioner for Refugees, 2003).

[6] Central Statistics Organization, *Afghanistan Statistical Yearbook 2003*; World Bank., *World Development Indicators Database*World Bank Group, 2009)

[7] Report of the Secretary General of the United Nations on the Situation in Afghanistan, March 18, 2002.

[8] Kabul Hindokosh in Dari 1400 GMT 5 Jan 04; IAP20040106000048. Kabul Radio Afghanistan in Pashto 1330 GMT 7 Jan 04; IAP20040107000110. Such claims are to be taken with a grain of salt: political parties played little role in Afghan politics in 2003 because there was no legislature. Kabul Radio Afghanistan in Pashto 1430 GMT 9 Jan 04; IAP20040109000086. Kabul Jowzjanan in Dari 0001 GMT 31 Jan 04, IAP20040218000008. Qala-e Naw Qala-e Naw Radio in Dari 0335 GMT 5 Jan 04; IAP20040108000122. Kabul Hewad in Pashto 8 Jan 04; IAP20040109000091 .

[9] The Asia Foundation, *Afghanistan in 2006: A Survey of the Afghan People.*

[10] *Donor Assistance Database Afghanistan,* Ministry of Finance, Islamic Republic of Afghanistan, 2009.

[11] International Monetary Fund

[12] Central Statistics Organization, *Afghanistan Statistical Yearbook 2003*; International Monetary Fund, *Islamic Republic of Afghanistan: Selected Issues and Statistical Appendix*

[13] The Secretary-General of the United Nations, *Report of the Secretary-General on the Situation in Afghanistan and its Implications for International Peace and Security* (New York: United Nations Security Council,[2005]).

[14] *Afghanistan Report 2009* (Brussels, Belgium: NATO,[2009]).

[15] *Afghanistan's Security Environment* (Washington, D.C.: U.S. Government Accountability Office,[2010]).

[16] Ralph Sundberg, "Collective Violence 2002 - 2007: Global and Regional Trends," in *States in Armed Conflict 2007*, eds. Lotta Harbom and Ralph Sundberg (Uppsala: Universitetstryckeriet, 2008).

[17] Seth G. Jones, "The Rise of Afghanistan's Insurgency: State Failure and Jihad," *International Security* 32, no. 4 (Spring 2008, 2008): 7-40.

[18] *ISAF Troops in Numbers (Placemat)*NATO,[2007-2009]).

[19] Report of the Secretary General of the United Nations on the Situation in Afghanistan, March 18, 2002.

[20] Sarah Lister, *Moving Forward? Assessing Public Administration Reform in Afghanistan* (Kabul: Afghan Research and Evaluation Unit,[2006]).

[21] Blue, *Assessment of the Impact of USAID Funded Technical Assistance-Capacity Building: Final Report*

[22] Lister, *Moving Forward?*

[23] The Secretary-General of the United Nations, *Report of the Secretary-General on the Situation in Afghanistan and its Implications for International Peace and Security* (New York: United Nations Security Council,[2006]).

[24] UNODC, *Afghanistan Opium Survey - Oct 2007,* United Nations Office on Drugs and Crime,[2007]).

[25] Catherine M. Trujillo, *Audit of USAID/Afghanistan's Capacity Development Program* (Manila: USAID Office of Inspector General,[2008]).

Chapter 5

[1] Enhanced Partnership with Pakistan Act of 2009. http://www.govtrack.us/congress/bills/111/s1707/text See Section 101(a) and Section 102(b).

[2] Enhanced Partnership with Pakistan Act of 2009. http://www.govtrack.us/congress/bills/111/s1707/text See Section 203(c)

[3] Omar Warrich, "How a U.S. Aid Package to Pakistan Could Threaten Zardari," *Time*, October 8, 2009. Available at http://www.time.com/time/world/article/0,8599,1929306,00.html accessed on June 27, 2012.

[4] Inter Services Public Relations, "Press Release: No PR396/2009-ISPR," October 7, 2009. Available at http://www.ispr.gov.pk/front/main.asp?o=t-press_release&id=914 accessed on June 27, 2012.

[5] Reidel, 107.

[6] Lieven, 5.

[7] Stephen P. Cohen, *The Idea of Pakistan*, Brookings Institution Press, 2004, pg. 196

[8] Shuja Nawaz, "Learning by Doing: The Pakistan Army's Experience with Counterinsurgency," The Atlantic Council, South Asia Center, February 2011.

[9] U.S. Overseas Loans and Grants, 1945 – 2010. http://gbk.eads.usaidallnet.gov/

[10] Congressional Research Service. http://www.fas.org/sgp/crs/row/pakaid.pdf

[11] Congressional Research Service.
http://www.fas.org/sgp/crs/row/pakaid.pdf
[12] Anatol Lieven, *Pakistan: A Hard Country*, (Public Affairs, 2011), pg. 97.
[13] Elisabeth Bumiller and Jane Perlez, "Pakistan's Spy Agency is Tied to Attack on US Embassy," *The New York Times,* September 22, 2011. http://www.nytimes.com/2011/09/23/world/asia/mullen-asserts-pakistani-role-in-attack-on-us-embassy.html?pagewanted=all
[14] Saeed Shah, "Pakistan defiant as U.S. cuts off $800 million in military aid," *McClatchy Newspapers*, July 10, 2011. Available at http://www.mcclatchydc.com/2011/07/10/117389/pakistan-defiant-as-us-cuts-off.html accessed on June 27, 2012.
[15] "U.S. cuts Pakistan aid over jailing of bin Laden sting doctor," *The Sunday Morning Herald*, May 25, 2012. Available at http://www.smh.com.au/world/us-cuts-pakistan-aid-over-jailing-of-bin-laden-sting-doctor-20120525-1z8tq.html accessed on June 27, 2012.
[16] United States Census Bureau, "Trade in Goods with Pakistan," http://www.census.gov/foreign-trade/balance/c5350.html ; CIA World Factbook 2012; Office of the United States Trade Representative, "U.S.-Pakistan trade facts," http://www.ustr.gov/countries-regions/south-central-asia/pakistan
[17] Code of Federal Regulations, 22 CFR 120.32 "Major Non-NATO Ally." http://www.law.cornell.edu/cfr/text/22/120/32
[18] "Mohammad's Capture Was Months in the Making," CNN.com, March 3, 2003. http://articles.cnn.com/2003-03-03/world/capture.tictoc_1_ahmed-abdul-qadoos-pakistani-police-qaeda?_s=PM:asiapcf
[19] Jane Perlez, "Drones Batter al-Qaida and its Allies Within Pakistan," *The New York Times*, April 4, 2010. http://www.nytimes.com/2010/04/05/world/asia/05drones.html
[20] Bruce Riedel, *Deadly Embrace*, Brookings Institution, 2010, pg. 13.
[21] Matthew Cole, "Killing Ourselves in Afghanistan," *Salon*, March 10, 2008.
[22] Syed Saleem Shahzad, "Baitullah: Dead or Alive, His Battle Rages," *The Asia Times Online*, August 8, 2009. http://www.atimes.com/atimes/South_Asia/KH08Df04.html ; Amir Mir, "Hakimullah Mehsud Evades U.S. Drones Again," *The Asia Times Online*, January 27, 2012. http://www.atimes.com/atimes/South_Asia/NA27Df01.html
[23] Candace Rondeaux, "Former Pakistani Intelligence Official Denies Aiding Group Ties to Mumbia Seige," *The Washington Post*, December 9, 2009; "Hamid Gul and LeT's Chachu may get official terrorist tag," *The Economic Times*, December 6, 2008.

http://articles.economictimes.indiatimes.com/2008-12-06/news/28411860_1_lashkar-militants-terror-attacks-yusuf-muzammil
[24] See, for example, H.R. 4228, introduced in March 2012.
[25] "Interservices Intelligence (ISI), *The New York Times*, Times Topics, updated March 9, 2012, reports that "Members of the ISI's shadowy S wing — which directs operations outside of Pakistan and helped create the Taliban — were seen as particularly close to militants."
http://topics.nytimes.com/top/reference/timestopics/organizations/i/interservices_intelligence/index.html
[26] Steve Coll, *Ghost Wars* and Ahmed Rashid *Descent into Chaos* both document these and other charges in detail.
[27] See the U.S. State Department's "Foreign Terrorist Organizations" website, http://www.state.gov/j/ct/rls/other/des/123085.htm
[28] *The Year of the Drone: An Analysis of U.S. Drone Strikes in Pakistan, 2004-2012*, The New America Foundation. Online resource and dataset. http://counterterrorism.newamerica.net/drones
[29] See Bob Woodward, *Obama's Wars*, page. 8, for the Angor Adda raid.
[30] "Suspected drone attack kills 4 in Pakistan," *New York Daily News*, March 30, 2012.
[31] Dan Lothian and Reza Sayah, "Obama's drone comment was no slip-up, officials say," CNN.com, January 31, 2012. http://articles.cnn.com/2012-01-31/politics/politics_obama-pakistan_1_drone-strikes-drone-missions-target-al?_s=PM:POLITICS

Chapter 6

[1] "Village Stability Operations ~ 101: Understanding USSOCOM's role in VSO and ALP in Afghanistan and Beyond," *The Donovan Review 2nd Edition*, US Special Operations Command, January 2012, pg. 6-7.
[2] Hy Rothstein, "America's Longest War," in *Afghan Endgames*, Hy Rothstein and John Arquilla, eds., pg. 77.
[3] S/2012/462, pg. 6. Report on Progress Toward Security and Stability in Afghanistan," U.S. Department of Defense, April 2012, pg. 63-66. http://www.defense.gov/pubs/pdfs/Report_Final_SecDef_04_27_12.pdf.
[4] "Report on Progress Toward Security and Stability in Afghanistan," U.S. Department of Defense, October 2011. http://www.defense.gov/pubs/pdfs/October_2011_Section_1230_Report.pdf
[5] S/2011/210, pg. 2.
[6] Carlotta Gall, "Losses in Pakistani Haven Strain Afghan Taliban," *New York Times*, March 31, 2011.
[7] Report on Progress Toward Security and Stability in Afghanistan," U.S. Department of Defense, April 2012,

http://www.defense.gov/pubs/pdfs/Report_Final_SecDef_04_27_12.pdf .
S/2012/462, pg. 4-5.

[8] "Declaration by the Heads of State and Government of the Nations contributing to the UN-mandated, NATO-led International Security Assistance Force (ISAF) in Afghanistan," Lisbon Summit, 20 November 2010. http://www.nato.int/cps/en/natolive/news_68722.htm

[9] "Chicago Summit Declaration on Afghanistan," Chicago Summit, 21 May 2012. http://www.nato.int/cps/en/natolive/official_texts_87595.htm

[10] "Enduring Strategic Partnership Agreement Between the United States of America and the Islamic Republic of Afghanistan." http://www.whitehouse.gov/sites/default/files/2012.06.01u.s.-afghanistanspasignedtext.pdf

[11] David W. Barno and Andrew Exum, "Responsible Transition: Security U.S. Interests in Afghanistan Beyond 2011," Center for a New American Security, December 2010, pg. 24.

[12] Report on Progress," U.S. Department of Defense, April 2012, pg. 1. S/2012/462, pg. 5.

[13] Barno, "Responsible Transition," pg. 26-28.

[14] "Report on Progress," U.S. Department of Defense, April 2012, pg. 6.

[15] "Quarterly Report to the U.S. Congress," Special Inspector General for Afghanistan Reconstruction, July 30, 2012. http://www.sigar.mil/pdf/quarterlyreports/2012-07-30qr.pdf

[16] S/2002/278.

[17] "Full Text of General Petraeus' testimony to Congress," March 15, 2011. http://www.longwarjournal.org/threat-matrix/archives/2011/03/full_text_of_general_petraeus.php

[18] Freya Peterson, "Hillary Clinton announces major non-NATO ally status for Afghanistan," globalpost.com, July 7, 2012. http://www.globalpost.com/dispatch/news/regions/asia-pacific/afghanistan/120707/afghanistan-nato-ally-status-hillary-clinton-kabul-hamid-karzai

[19] http://www.ctapafghanistan.org/en/overview.html

[20] James Risen, "US Identifies Vast Mineral Riches in Afghanistan," New York Times, June 13, 2010.